Child's Play

Child's Play

Revisiting Play in Early Childhood Settings

MAIN EDITOR: **Elizabeth Dau,**
Dip. Teach. (Early Childhood), B. Ed.
Lecturer, Regency TAFE, South Australia and early childhood consultant

CONSULTING EDITOR: **Dr. Elizabeth Jones,**
M.A. (Child Development), Ph.D. (Sociology)
*Faculty of Human Development, Pacific Oaks College,
Pasadena, California*

·PAUL·H·
BROOKES
PUBLISHING C<u>O</u>

Baltimore • London • Toronto • Sydney

Paul H. Brookes Publishing Co.
Post Office Box 10624
Baltimore, Maryland 21285-0624

www.brookespublishing.com

© 1999 MacLennan & Petty Pty Limited
All rights reserved.
First published for exclusive distribution in North America by
Paul H. Brookes Publishing Co. in July 2001.

National Library of Australia Cataloguing-in-Publication data
are available from the National Library of Australia.

ISBN 1-55766-573-7

Printed and bound in the United States of America by
Lightning Source, Inc., LaVergne, Tennessee.

Endorsed by the
Australian Early Childhood Association

Contents

Foreword   xi
About the Editors   xv
About the Contributors   xvii
Acknowledgments   xx
Preface   xxi

Part 1: Play, Development and Learning   **1**

Introduction   3

Chapter 1 The role of play in development and learning   5
Anne Glover
    Introduction   5
    Play from a constructivist perspective   6
    Implications for development and learning   8
    Conclusion   12
    For further thought and discussion   14

Chapter 2 Stop, look and listen: adopting an investigative
stance when children play   16
Elspeth Harley
    Introduction   16
    Play: a personal anecdote   17
    The developmental paradigm of play   19
    The role of the early childhood educator   23
    Conclusion   26
    For further thought and discussion   26

Chapter 3 Thinking about play, playing about thinking   28
Sue Dockett
    Introduction   28
    Defining play   31

Observing and interpreting play   32
Play as a cognitive and social experience   32
Alternative views of play   36
Playing with thinking   41
Conclusion   43
For further thought and discussion   43

Part 2: Play and Diversity   **47**

Introduction   49

Chapter 4 Developmentally appropriate play and
turtle hunting   53
Lyn Fasoli

Introduction   53
The first locations: the original agenda   53
A new location: the script changes   54
Conclusion   57
For further thought and discussion   58

Chapter 5 Aboriginal children and play   60
Veronica Johns

Introduction   60
Planning for play   60
Characteristics of Aboriginal children's play   61
Conclusion   66
For further thought and discussion   66

Chapter 6 Universal fantasy: the domination of Western
theories of play   67
Marilyn Fleer

Introduction   68
The play activities of children   68
Paradigm shifts in the conceptualisation of play   69
The learning of play   70
Characteristics of Western and non-Western
    play activities   73

The implications for educators 76
Conclusion 77
For further thought and discussion 78

Chapter 7 Even pink tents have glass ceilings: crossing
the gender boundaries in pretend play 81
Glenda MacNaughton

Introduction 81
Pretend play and power 81
Playing across the gender boundaries 85
Minimising the risks of crossing the gender boundaries 91
The value of pretend play 91
Conclusion 93
For further thought and discussion 94

Chapter 8 Play and the gifted child 97
Cathie Harrison and Kim Tegel

Introduction 97
Characteristics of the gifted child 98
Play patterns of the gifted child 99
Play: a context for learning 101
The role of the supportive adult 102
Conclusion 108
For further thought and discussion 109

Chapter 9 The place of play for young children
with disabilities in mainstream education 111
Barbara Creaser

Introduction 111
School One: an example of a school for children
with severe disabilities 113
School Two: an example of a school with a 50 per cent
disability rate 114
Discussion 125
Conclusion 128
For further thought and discussion 130

Part 3: The Play Environment, Resources and the Adult's Role   **131**

Introduction   133

Chapter 10 A walk around Lucy's garden: a playground designed to foster children's play and enhance learning   137
Pauline Berry

    Introduction   137
    Redeveloping a playground   137
    Features of the new design   139
    Conclusion   149
    For further thought and discussion   150

Chapter 11 Play, a way of being for babies and toddlers   152
Anne Stonehouse

    Introduction   152
    The essence of play for babies and toddlers   154
    How play fits into a group program for babies
        and toddlers   154
    The basis of the program for babies and toddlers   155
    Differences in play for babies and toddlers   156
    The role of parents in contributing to play in day care   158
    Planning for children's play   158
    Important ingredients for the 'backdrop' to play   159
    Multiculturalism and anti-bias in play for under three-
        year-olds   160
    Conclusion   161
    For further thought and discussion   162

Chapter 12 Persona dolls: the effects on attitudes and play   164
Kerry Bosisto and Anne Howard

    Main Editor's interview with Kerry and Anne   164
    Introduction   167
    How we started   168
    Data collection   168
    Interviews with parents   171
    Staff involvement   172
    Parent involvement   172

Structure of sessions   173
Findings   175
Conclusion   179
For further thought and discussion   180

Chapter 13 'I can be playful too': the adult's role
in children's socio-dramatic play   187
Elizabeth Dau
Introduction   187
Observing children's socio-dramatic play   189
Planning for socio-dramatic play   192
The value of real-life experiences   194
Making time for socio-dramatic play   196
Necessary materials and resources   197
Conclusion   201
For further thought and discussion   201

Appendix: Exploring the correlation between *Child's Play*
and the National Child Care Competency Standards   203

Index   210

Foreword

This book represents, to me, the continuation of many warm and stimulating relationships. My most recent of many visits to Australia was for the launch, in Adelaide, 1995, of Barbara Creaser and Elizabeth Dau's book, *The Anti-Bias Approach in Early Childhood*—also the occasion of a memorial to my friend, Barb. Barb's chapter in this book was written some years ago while she was studying in the States, during which time I accompanied her to the Washington State Early Childhood Conference, where she presented it. I have been thinking ever since about her observations on children with special needs and how their play is so often interrupted.

Other memories I share with the contributors of this book include sitting on the grass at Elspeth Harley's centre, watching children's extraordinary construction of a 'mine'; being introduced first-hand by Pauline Berry to an irresistible outdoor play space she had designed; reading Sue Dockett's dissertation and stimulating analyses of children's thinking about their play, and corresponding with her about them; and visiting preschools in Fiji with Anne Glover where, as always, we talked incessantly. I only wish I had been part of Lyn Fasoli's turtle hunt—the stuff of which dreams are made!

I haven't met Kerry Bosisto or Anne Howard, but I'm grateful to both for enhancing my earlier understanding, gained from colleagues in my home town of Los Angeles, about the proper uses of persona dolls. In *Anti-Bias Curriculum: Tools for Empowering Young Children* (by Derman-Sparks and the Anti-Bias Task Force), Kay Taus describes how she kept her persona dolls on top of the piano so that children would understand how special they were, and not see them as just ordinary playthings—though they could ask permission to play with them. Kerry and Anne, by contrast, invite the children to make friends with the dolls, who 'go everywhere with the children'—even home overnight because, these teachers reason, 'there will be greater acceptance of the dolls and potentially, therefore, of diversity.' What a fine example of taking up a tradition invented by someone else, and improving upon it with your own good idea!

With these friends and others I am 'playing'—in the ways professionals need to—with experiences, words and ideas to increase our understanding of our work, and of the unexpected issues it keeps raising. Through reading, writing and e-mail, we can even play with people we've never met face-to-face; professional networks extend around the world. Professionals who stop 'playing' get stale; such teachers dust off their curriculum every year and recycle it with their latest group of learners. The learners may not guess that it's old stuff—but the teachers, I suspect, know, and may wonder if this is why they find teaching less challenging and inspiring than in their early days when they were less practised.

Our own early childhood is a window of opportunity for learning to play; if we miss it then, or get it trained out of us later, we will be less competent as adults in carrying out complex, unpredictable tasks. Teaching is, in fact, among the most unpredictable of human endeavours—and the learners do their best to keep it that way!

'How did you play as a child?' This is a question I put to many adults; it's one of the best questions I know. I was surprised, therefore, in a group of Australian teacher educators, when one of them insisted that she *didn't* play as a child. Her colleagues, who knew her better than I did, weren't surprised. Her inability to play as an adult—to be flexible in collective problem solving, for instance—made her difficult to work with. They regretted her play-less childhood, even though she, to all appearances, did not. Perhaps she didn't know what she was missing.

Marilyn Fleer's provocative chapter argues that play, as defined in the other chapters in this book, is not a universal phenomenon but rather a learnt behaviour. She cites cross-cultural research to support this premise, and states that children play in those societies where adults think it is important, or at least harmless. Glenda Mac-Naughton's chapter takes this a step further and calls play dangerous. Indeed, play *can* be dangerous; it encourages unconventional thinking and behaviour.

However, play is also how people get smart. In a conservative society, rigid and resistant to change, smart people—people who ask questions and suggest alternative ways of approaching problems—are often perceived as a nuisance, so often only that play which directly imitates adult behaviour is tolerated. Children everywhere play at being grown-up and, in a society lacking in a variety of adult roles, play will be less elaborate. However, in a diverse and rapidly changing society (which includes not only Australia, but most of the world at the turn of the century) smart people are, more than ever, a necessity. An increasing number of children face the challenge of becoming bi-culturally competent—that is, able to meet different expectations at home and at school—which demands that they get smart and are able to find a workable balance between those expectations. There are many problems to be solved at both personal and societal levels, and complex problem solving depends on the ideas of people who don't take certain traditions—such as war, poverty, bias and oppression—for granted, but ask the hard questions and play with the possibility of finding fresh solutions.

School, as I remember it from my childhood, is where you don't get to play. Even later as a parent, I was sternly reminded by the teacher of my playful five-year-old daughter that 'the children must learn that kindergarten is not nursery school'. Yet I like to play, and I would never have become a teacher if I hadn't discovered preschool, where I could sit on the floor and watch young children playing. I've been learning from children at play ever since, and have become convinced that early childhood education is the best teaching–learning model to be found anywhere. Adults, like children, learn through play: through choosing challenging activities, investigating the possibilities they offer, and creating still more possibilities in collaboration with other players. In a diverse and rapidly changing world, the capacity to 'brainstorm'—to dream the impossible and play with the possible—offers our best hope that we might learn to live together, to create a more peaceful society in which the differences among us stimulate interest and pleasure, rather than fear and anger.

It is not surprising, therefore, that the books I value most are those that tell memorable stories (just as play does), and *Child's Play* presents a fine collection of such stories about children's play in Australia. Reading them, you will encounter Andrew the horse, Mary and the magic control panel, Sasha and the sword-mermaid, Chloe and her pink tent, Long Long finding a lizard, Damien in his fireman's hat, and many more. With them are playful teachers, interacting not only with the children but also with us, the readers, offering us the intellectual stimulus essential to our continuing growth as thoughtful teachers and adults. Their reflections invite us, too, to ask ourselves:

- What can we learn about children by observing their play?
- Is play disappearing from children's daily lives?
- In our eagerness to 'teach' children, are we interfering with what they could be learning through play?
- Are there dangers inherent in play, and if so, how can we help make it fair and safe?

- Should adults involve themselves in children's socio-dramatic play?
- Is a curriculum that emphasises imaginative play inappropriate for children from non-Western cultures?

What do *you* think? Read the thoughts and experiences of the contributors in this book, and play with the ideas they offer!

Dr Elizabeth (Betty) Jones
Pacific Oaks College
Pasadena, California

Reference

Derman-Sparks, L. & the Anti-Bias Task Force 1989, *Anti-Bias Curriculum: Tools for Empowering Young Children*, National Association for the Education of Young Children, Washington DC.

About the Editors

Elizabeth Dau (Main Editor)

Elizabeth Dau holds a Dip. Teach. (Early Childhood) and B. Ed. She is a part-time lecturer at the Regency TAFE (Elizabeth Campus), South Australia and an early childhood consultant. Her previous positions include various posts in the ACT schools system, Assistant National Director of the Australian Early Childhood Association and Program Manager of the Northern Territory Children's Services Resource and Advisory Program, a program which supported child care services throughout the Territory. Elizabeth came to South Australia from her position as Head of the Child Studies Department at the Canberra Institute of Technology.

Elizabeth's major interests are anti-bias and play, in particular socio-dramatic play.

Elizabeth has published widely and her publications include *Ladies can't be Bus Drivers: Addressing Issues of Diversity with Young Children; Developing Effective Work Teams; Partnership with Parents; Anti-Bias—What does it have to do with Me?; Who's Celebrations? Some Questions to Consider; Who's in Charge of Celebrations? A Child Centred Approach* (with Barbara Creaser); 'Let's Pretend', in *The Arts in Early Childhood* edited by S. Wright; *Drama for Young Children*; and *The Anti-Bias Approach in Early Childhood* which she edited with Barbara Creaser.

Dr Elizabeth Jones (Consulting Editor)

Betty Jones is a member of the Faculty of Human Development of Pacific Oaks College and Children's Programs in Pasadena, California, where she taught both adults and children. She holds an M.A. in Child Development and a Ph.D. in Sociology. Her recent studies have focused on teacher education and adult learning, emergent curriculum, and on the development of play, language and literacy in children.

Betty has been a visiting lecturer at the University of Alaska and in 1986 was a De Lissa Fellow at the University of South Australia. She is the author of many articles and books, including *Dimensions of Teaching—Learning Environments* and *Teaching Adults: An Active Learning Approach*. She collaborated with Australian John Nimmo on emergent curriculum, and with Gretchen Reynolds wrote *The Play's the Thing: Teachers' Roles in Children's Play* and *Master Players: Learning from Children at Play*.

About the Contributors

Pauline Berry, Dip. Teach. (Early Childhood), B. Ed. (Early Childhood), is an early childhood consultant. Her special interests and areas of work are children's play and the development of outdoor play environments designed to meet the needs and interests of young children. She has been a teacher of young children, a Director of a number of early childhood centres and a Coordinator in the South Australian Children's Services Office, working with staff, families and the community. She has also worked with student teachers for many years, particularly in the area of field experience. She has researched and published various papers, including 'Children's use of fixed equipment' and 'Playing with print' as well as an evaluation program, 'Parent involvement in a kindergarten'.

Kerry Bosisto, Dip. Teach. (ECE), B. Ed. (ECE), is Director at J. B. Cleland Kindergarten in Adelaide and has worked in kindergartens across the range of socio-economic areas over the past 18 years. The anti-bias curriculum has provided her with a framework for addressing issues of special interest—social justice, global education, and racial and gender equity. She has especially enjoyed working with her peers on the action research described in Chapter 12, 'Persona dolls: the effects on attitudes and play'. Having seen its benefits at first hand, Kerry has great confidence in, and commitment to, the anti-bias approach.

Barbara Creaser (1940–1995), Dip. T. (KTC), Diploma Child Development, M.A. in Human Development, held positions including Senior Lecturer in Early Childhood Education and Child Care Studies at the Northern Territory University, Adviser to preschools with the Kindergarten Union of South Australia, and various posts in South Australian, interstate and overseas preschools. She worked as a consultant in care and education in the Australian Capital Territory.

Sue Dockett, B. Ed. (Early Childhood), M. Ed. (Hons), Ph.D., is an Associate Professor in the Faculty of Education at the University of Western Sydney. Sue developed a research program related to young children's thinking which extended through her M. Ed. and Ph.D. into continuing projects. This interest is reflected in a number of her publications and in Chapter 3 of this book, 'Thinking about play, playing about thinking'. Sue has published widely and her publications on play are much respected. She is also known to students of early childhood in TAFE organisations and universities for her part in the publication *Programming and Planning in Early Childhood Settings*, now in its second edition.

Lyn Fasoli, B.Sc. (ECE), M. Sc., is currently a Senior Lecturer in early childhood at the Northern Territory University. She has extensive experience in early childhood in a variety of roles and contexts, including lecturer in Australia and overseas in child care studies and early childhood teacher education. Lyn has a keen interest in how children learn in informal learning environments, focusing on children's museums. Her research has covered children's play and planning for learning through play. In her current research she adopts a narrative enquiry approach to explore how Aboriginal early childhood practitioners teach young Aboriginal children.

Marilyn Fleer, Dip. Teach. (Early Childhood), B. Ed., M. Ed. (Hons), Ph.D., is Associate Professor in Education at the University of Canberra. Marilyn has taught in preschool and child care, has been a Curriculum Officer, Early Childhood Adviser and Senior Research Officer. Her research includes early childhood science and technology education, cross-cultural issues and play, and theories of how children think and learn. She has published widely and her research interests are reflected in many of her publications, including Chapter 6 of this book, 'Universal fantasy: the domination of Western theories of play'.

Anne Glover, Dip. T. (KTC), B. Ed., Grad. Dip. Parent Education and Counselling, M.A., is currently working in Papua New Guinea as the Team Leader of an Australian Aid project supporting the development of elementary education. Prior to this, she was the Coordinator of Early Childhood Education at the University of the South Pacific and has recently completed a consultancy reviewing UNICEF's Pacific Basic Education Program. Anne is on extended leave from her position as Senior Lecturer in the de Lissa Institute of Early Childhood and Family Studies at the University of South Australia. Her research and writing activities have focused on issues relating to racism, Aboriginality, bi-cultural development, anti-bias curriculum and the play of young children.

Elspeth Harley, Dip. T. (KTC), B. Ed., is a curriculum officer with the South Australian Department of Education, Training and Employment, and has been involved in the development and writing of two early childhood curriculum frameworks. As an early childhood teacher and drama teacher she has taught in preschool and the first years of school. She has a strong interest in young children and the media, and is a Director of Young Media Australia. She has a passionate interest in children's play and is currently completing her Masters degree by research into a therapeutic model of play.

Cathie Harrison, B. Ed. (Early Childhood), M. Ed. (specialising in gifted children), lectures at the University of Western Sydney, Macarthur, in the early childhood program. Her areas of teaching include children's play, visual arts, and programming and planning in early childhood settings. She is the author of the book *Giftedness in Early Childhood*, published by the Kindergarten Union Children's Services, and is involved in lecturing and consultancy in the field of gifted education.

Anne Howard, Dip. T. (ECE), B. Ed.(Sp. Ed.), has worked in both country and city preschools for 20 years and is currently teacher at J. B. Cleland Kindergarten in Adelaide. She is particularly interested in social skills and has undertaken action research and written a curriculum document for the South Australian Department of Education, Employment and Training. Anne has recently been involved in an action research project on anti-bias curriculum and the use of persona dolls.

Veronica Johns holds an Associate Diploma in Child Care Studies from the Northern Territory University. She is Director of Jalygurr Guwan (Children of the Pearl), a Multifunctional Aboriginal Children's Service in Broome. Previously, she was the Aboriginal Children's Services Coordinator at the Northern Territory Children's Services Resource and Advisory Program, Darwin. Veronica is the co-author of *From the Flat Earth: A Guide for Child Care Staff Caring for Aboriginal Children*, and author of the chapter 'Empowering adults—a personal experience' in *The Anti-Bias Approach in Early Childhood*, edited by Barbara Creaser and Elizabeth Dau.

Glenda MacNaughton, Dip. Teach. (Early Childhood), B. Ed., Diploma Early Childhood Studies, Ph.D., is a Senior Lecturer in the Department of Early Childhood at the University of Melbourne. She has a strong interest in social justice and equity issues in early childhood. She has published widely on these issues and, together with Gillian Williams, has recently completed *Techniques for Teaching Young Children: Choices in Theory and Practice*.

Anne Stonehouse, B.A. (Psychology), M.A. (Child Psychology), is currently Associate Professor of Early Childhood at Monash University. She has served as the National President of the Australian Early Childhood Association and is the author of numerous books and publications, including *How Does it Feel? Child Care from a Parent's Perspective, Trusting Toddlers, Not Just Nice Ladies, Ourselves in Their Shoes, Opening the Doors: Child Care in a Multicultural Society* and, most recently, *Prime Times: a Handbook for Excellence in Infant and Toddler Programs*, co-authored with Jim Greenman.

Kim Tegel, B. Ed. (Early Childhood), M. Ed. (Teaching Gifted Children), lectures at the University of Western Sydney, Macarthur, in the early childhood program. Among the subjects she teaches are Child Growth and Development, Play, and Gifted Education. She has a commitment to supporting all children, particularly those who are gifted, their families and educators so that all children may reach their full potential.

Acknowledgments

From the moment I thought of editing a book on children's play, Elizabeth (Betty) Jones gave me support and encouragement. By agreeing to be the Consulting Editor, as well as writing the foreword, she convinced me that this book was possible. Firstly, therefore, my thanks go to Betty, a very special person, and mentor to many people working in the field of early childhood in various parts of the world.

The contributors also deserve special thanks. To some, publishing is relatively new; others have a great deal of experience. You have all been wonderful and have written chapters that are both informative and challenging—and well worth the research involved. I extend my heartfelt thanks to all of you.

A special thank you also to Jill Huntley for your reading and comments—and patience. It has been particularly helpful to have someone who is such a clear thinker to read and comment on the contributors' chapters and also my own writing.

Debbie Lee's involvement in the preparation and publishing processes of *The Anti-Bias Approach in Early Childhood* was really appreciated. As we say in the acknowledgments section in that book: 'We do want to single out Debbie Lee for special thanks for her bubbling energy and enthusiasm and the wonderful way she has led us through what originally felt like a daunting project.' These comments apply equally to this publication. Thank you again, Debbie.

Reference

Creaser, B. and Dau, E. (eds), 1995, *The Anti-Bias Approach in Early Childhood*, HarperEducational, Sydney.

Preface

When I started to think about editing a book on children's play for staff in child care situations and students of early childhood, I decided to talk to a Child Care Centre Director whom I had known in the past. I knew that at that time she had had a commitment to fostering children's pretend play. I asked Chris if she was still offering a play-based curriculum. I remember clearly the astonishment in her voice when she responded, 'is there any other way?'

It was reassuring for me to find, at a time when it appears that the concept of play is becoming undervalued, a director whose commitment to it hasn't wavered.

I wanted to talk to Chris because, when conducting in-service on play as the basis of program planning, I sometimes hear comments such as, 'we don't have the time that it takes', 'we can't afford all the materials', or 'it all sounds too hard'. I asked Chris if she found it hard to maintain a program with play as the basis. She laughed and said, 'If staff would only read about it, go to in-service sessions and try it they would soon discover just how easy it is!' To illustrate her point, she told me the following story.

> Now I am a Director of a Service I have less time with the children than previously, although I have some time each day and only an emergency would stop me having that. I recall one day when I was in the office catching up on the ubiquitous paperwork and I heard quite loud voices outside. I went out to investigate. There were two relatively new members of staff trying to entice some boys inside to do some table activities even though we have an open-door program so children can be wherever it suits their play. One of the two staff members commented that they were having difficulty 'controlling' this particular group of boys. I suggested that they involve them in some type of play. 'I don't know where to start with that. It all seems far too hard,' she responded.
>
> I knew that one of these boys had recently been camping so I went to the storeroom and brought out some props and said, picking up a frying pan, some red cellophane and a few blocks, 'I think it is nearly

tea time and I'm hungry! I'd better get the fire going and cook some sausages. I'll need someone to help me with the fire.'

It was just a short time later that I was able to withdraw and observe the play—one child cooking tea, two fishing and one putting the baby to bed.

I made a mental note that I needed to do a lot more training with these new staff members. I believe, very strongly, that children learn through play.

Children and adults playing together is a sight I used to enjoy when I visited Chris in her place of work. I am concerned that now I see it far less often. Instead, I usually see children being moved *away* from play towards more traditional, school-like experiences. There are many factors contributing to this trend which I, and a number of the contributors in this book, see as a move away from play. I believe the two major factors are:

1. The importance that our increasingly competitive society is placing on achieving professional success, and the consequent desire of families to prepare their children for that success.
2. The resulting pressure on staff from their perceived need to be seen by the parents as teaching their children—and producing the evidence.

I believe that, in order for play to resume its rightful place in our early childhood settings, staff in those settings—be they child care, preschools or schools—need:

1. Assistance in gaining confidence that play is the way children learn best. Part 1 of this book presents very clearly the argument that play is developmentally appropriate for young children and should be an integral part of every child's day. Part 2, which addresses issues related to diversity, also supports the notion of play as a valuable learning experience for *all* children. In Part 3, readers are encouraged to—and supported in—introducing play as a basis of their programs.
2. Help in understanding that children can be trusted to direct their own play. I am not suggesting that adults do not, at times, need to intervene or participate in children's play. Chapter 7 by Glenda

MacNaughton, for instance, sets out clearly instances when such intervention becomes necessary.

3. Encouragement to be playful themselves! What a joy it was to watch Chris being playful with children and contributing to their enjoyment. Playfulness can be of immense benefit if it is carried into adulthood.

4. Assistance in communicating the value of play to families and indeed the community in general.

5. In-service training to help put the above points into practice.

While intended primarily for staff at early childhood centres, preschools and the early years of school and students of early childhood, this book will also be of use to lecturers and teachers who train students. It will also be relevant to parents and families, and those interested in early childhood. As an adult in children's lives, you have— or will have if you are a student—an enormous impact. You provide their environment and control it, and thus have considerable control over their interactions and behaviour, and the messages they receive. In the words of a colleague of mine: 'This is a plea for play'.

The various chapters in this book will:

- inspire you;
- challenge your thinking;
- caution you;
- introduce you to the diversity that exists in our services and explain what this means in terms of children's play;
- give practical suggestions for establishing environments for play;
- reinforce that what you are doing in relation to play is appropriate and the best possible option for the children in your care.

Finally, I draw your attention to the Appendix, a unique feature of this book. Helen Gibson, who was the Curriculum Officer at the Canberra Institute of Technology for two years and responsible for the development of the National Child Care Curriculum, has matched the nationally agreed Child Care Competencies to the content of this book. The resulting matrix will be of assistance to all those working in child care training as we move towards meeting the national competencies.

Elizabeth Dau
Regency TAFE
South Australia

Part 1

PLAY, DEVELOPMENT AND LEARNING

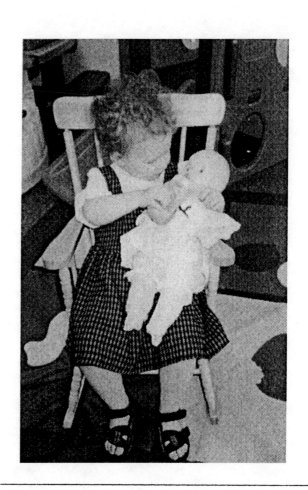

Part 1

Play, Development and Learning

Young children are active learners who construct their own understanding and knowledge of the world. Play is an essential aspect of learning for young children, and planning for play is the central component in developing a curriculum that integrates all areas of a child's development. Early childhood educators have a critical role in responding to children's play ideas and in establishing an environment which supports and extends their learning and development through play. (For a more detailed explanation, see *Foundation Areas of Learning*, p. 19.)

In Chapter 1 Anne Glover explores children's learning and development through play, providing us with an introduction to Part 1 and leading us into the rest of the book. Anne explores in detail the relationship between play, learning and development, themes which are taken up by later chapters. She employs a constructivist framework to examine the role of play in furthering children's social, emotional, cognitive and physical development. In the constructivist view, children's active participation in play is important in their construction of knowledge. When children engage in rich and meaningful play, they are learning how to be competent in our complicated, contemporary world. They are actively transforming experience into meaningful knowledge and mastering new skills and concepts. Anne suggests that without ample opportunities to engage in play, children's development and learning may be hampered. Chapter 13 takes this point up when it looks at children whose preferred mode of learning is socio-dramatic play.

Chapter 2, by Elspeth Harley, advocates adopting an investigative stance towards children's play. Rather than considering play from the perspective of children's social, emotional, cognitive and physical development, as Anne Glover does, Elspeth examines play through the developmental stages from first play to symbolic and dramatic play. She presents a framework, and a developmental paradigm, for early childhood staff who wish to understand more fully a developmental perspective on children's dramatic play in particular. This paradigm gives staff a tool for observing, assessing and evaluating children's play. (Sue Dockett, in Chapter 3, presents an alternative tool, and tools for use when observing and planning for children's play are also featured in Part 3.) Elspeth briefly raises the idea that children's capacity to play and dramatise will be dependent upon, among other things, the culture to which they belong. (Marilyn Fleer explores this idea further in Chapter 6.)

Chapter 3, by Sue Dockett, is based on the paper she wrote when she presented the inaugural Barbara Creaser Memorial Lecture (see the Main Editor's note at the beginning of Chapter 3). She opens her discussion with an example of children's play, 'Wombat Stew', and continues to use anecdotes throughout to illustrate her points, as does Elspeth Harley. Sue raises questions about the way play is often recorded and interpreted, and questions the theorists whose work forms the basis of our understanding about children's play. She proposes 'some different ways of thinking about play and recognising the playing with thinking in which children engage'.

Another point made in this chapter, and taken up in later chapters, is that play is something that is controlled by children, and while there may be times when it is appropriate for adults to intervene, generally adults are best observing. Some writers agree but others, such as Glenda MacNaughton in Chapter 7, present a case for more prompt adult intervention, as does Elspeth Harley in Chapter 2 when she says (although for reasons different to Glenda's) that play without adult support and involvement can be an 'aimless activity'.

Glenda MacNaughton, Marilyn Fleer and other writers challenge, like Sue Dockett, the conventional wisdom that surrounds children's play in Part 2, Play and Diversity. The adult's role in children's play is explored in greater depth in Part 3.

Sue Dockett suggests that 'we tend to value overseas research more readily than the contribution that has come from our own colleagues'. Some of the research in this book has 'come from our own colleagues' and will, I believe, make a significant contribution to our thinking and debate about children's play.

Reference

Department for Education and Children's Services 1996, *Foundation Areas of Learning: A Curriculum Framework*, Department for Education and Children's Services, Adelaide.

Chapter 1

The role of play in development and learning

Anne Glover

Introduction

Early childhood educators have long recognised the importance of play in young children's lives. Most would agree that play serves an important function in promoting healthy development and learning, and there would be very few, if any, early childhood programs in Australia that do not include a play component. Furthermore, as research increasingly demonstrates the significance of play in children's development, 'the commitment to encouraging the practice of play grows' (Kagan 1990).

Despite this growing commitment, an increasing number of writers are expressing concern about the devaluing and even the potential disappearance of play. It is argued that young children are being given less time to play (Elkind 1987); that play is being displaced by other activities including watching television and participating in organised sports (Evans 1995); and that our changing physical and social environments limit children's play opportunities (Elkind 1981; Postman 1982; Evans 1995). It is suggested that play is rapidly being replaced by commercial entertainment and recreation, and that adults, including parents, teachers and policy-makers, are placing increasingly less value on children's play. In short, there is concern that childhood play is being seriously undermined (Levin 1996).

This concern is based on the premiss that without adequate opportunities for play, young children's development and learning will be seriously hampered. As parents are being encouraged to teach infants and very young children to read, do maths and engage in a variety of formal non-playful activities, and many teachers feel pressured to emphasise and accelerate children's academic programs, there is mounting concern that children are being placed in inappropriate situations which will, paradoxically, put their learning at risk for no real purpose (Elkind 1987). As children spend more hours watching television and videos and less time outside playing with neighbours, building cubbyhouses, riding bikes and exploring back streets, parks and creeks, many worry that their physical and social development is also being put at risk.

Are these concerns justified? What are the implications for children's development and learning if they do not have adequate opportunities to engage in rich and meaningful play?

Play from a contructivist perspective

A constructivist view of early childhood posits that children build knowledge and skills through a slow and continuous process of construction (Levin 1996). As children actively explore their world, they build on what they already know and do in order to gain new understandings and skills. With each new encounter or interaction, new meanings are discovered, and more complex skills are developed.

Levin (1996) suggests that as children play and try things out, they encounter new or unexpected things. As this new information or situation doesn't quite fit into what they already know, they first experience confusion, then try to figure out or master the new content by adjusting their current ideas to it. In doing so, they learn something new, thereby reaching a new level of comfort. When this happens, they immediately try out their new skills until they encounter yet another challenge. According to Levin, the play process, which is an integral part of learning and development, involves the following steps:

- playing with what is already mastered or known;
- encountering an interesting problem to solve during play;
- solving or mastering the problem in play;
- having a new concept or skill to work on in play;
- playing with what has been learned or mastered.

(Levin 1996)

Through this process of interaction with their environment, children acquire competence in dealing with the physical and social world. They develop increasingly sophisticated and meaningful understandings and skills as they solve problems and meet new challenges. If we think about how young children learn language, or how they learn about numbers or science, the process becomes clearer. Children learn the 'twoness' of two, the 'threeness' of three, the way words join to make sentences, and how leaves float down when you throw them in the air, not passively or in isolation, but as a result of an ongoing experience. Each new interaction or experience results in information either being put into an existing framework of understanding, or causing a new framework to be created. More complex and refined understandings are being constructed from what is already known.

Early childhood educators who adhere to a constructivist view recognise children as active constructors of knowledge, not merely passive recipients of information. Far from the idea of children being 'blank slates' or 'empty vessels', children are viewed as active constructors of their own meaning through systematic assembling of the information they receive:

> Children do not just passively take in information from the world around them and learn it; rather, they actively transform it into something that is unique and personally meaningful. They use their experience as the context for building new meanings and skills onto what they have already learnt. (Levin 1996, p. 74)

From a constructivist perspective, play is an important part of the process of constructing knowledge for young children. Play provides a mechanism allowing them to move from what they already know and can master to more advanced knowledge. It allows them to control what happens and use what they know in their own unique ways to further their understandings and development (Levin 1996).

A two-year-old shuffles through the autumn leaves, bends down and takes a small handful, throws them in the air. They flutter down, he watches. Another handful in the air, then another and another—he is feeling the power of knowing how to do something interesting. Now he kicks a pile of leaves, none go in the air. Another kick, then another—still no leaves in the air. How to do it? A problem to be worked out, and some new information that doesn't fit into what is already known. The child, using what he already knows and has mastered, encounters an interesting problem and begins to solve it.

Implications for development and learning

Play begins as an exploration of the physical world (Jones & Reynolds, 1992). Young children, full of curiosity, learn about their world by touching, tasting and smelling that which they encounter:

> Kept safe by watchful adults, the competent toddler is a vigorous explorer of and with her own body and what it can do, of other people and their reactions, and of the world of interesting things all around. She pokes and dumps and pulls, tastes and smells and strokes whatever she encounters, increasingly adding verbal commentary in order to communicate with others and to reflect her own experiences. (Jones & Reynolds 1992, p. 2)

Gradually, 'knowing becomes more than sensory' (Jones & Reynolds, 1992) as children represent their experiences in order to understand them. Preschoolers represent their experiences in constructive, dramatic and socio-dramatic play—roads are built, dams are dug, fires are extinguished and babies fed. Children use oral and body language, art materials and wood, blocks and construction toys to recreate their experiences and, in doing so, make their world more meaningful:

> It is in this stage that the child first becomes a competent representor of experience rather than simply a doer of it. Human society and human thought are built on the achievement of representation, which makes possible both looking back and looking ahead, rather than simply living in the moment, and communication removed in both place and time, rather than simply face-to-face. The exploration of the toddler is direct encounter, not representation. But the dramatic play of four and five year-olds is increasingly sophisticated representations of both real and imagined experiences. (Jones & Reynolds 1992, p. 4)

Learning and development is advanced when children, representing their experiences, meet new and interesting problems and try to solve them—how to stop the tower from falling over, what to do with this big drop of paint which has landed in the middle of the paper, how to divide up the dough so that everyone gets some, and how to get a turn at being mum. Learning and development is also advanced as children try to master something a little more difficult than what they can already do—making the paint lines meet to create a house, cutting around the circle, using the tyre-swing.

When children are involved in play that allows them to explore and then represent their world, endless opportunities arise for them to further their cognitive, social, emotional and physical development in an integrated, holistic way (Levin 1996).

Social development and play

Play with their peers allows young children to build their social understandings and relationships. To each new situation, they bring what they have already learnt about being with others. As they encounter new and interesting relationships and problems, they extend their skills as they discover which social approaches work and which don't, how to sustain relationships, how to solve problems without using force or retreating and how to achieve mutually satisfying play.

One of the important aspects of children's social development during early childhood is the development of peer relationships. Children learn to socialise outside the family and engage in interactions with friends of the same-age group (Gordon & Browne 1993). Play with peers allows children to practise and extend what they already know about sharing, taking turns, exercising self-control, working in a group, cooperating and just plain getting along with others!

In socio-dramatic play, particularly, children are drawn into contact with one another. Much of their social repertoire is gained by engaging in dramatic play with other children (Gordon & Browne 1993). With each interaction, children use what they have already mastered and, as new and interesting situations arise, try out new behaviour. Socio-dramatic play is a perfect avenue for testing and extending social behaviour. It is, of course, not the only way that children learn the rules for social behaviour—they also learn by imitation and by direct teaching—but, as Jones observes, it is in dramatic play that children can practise, improvise and test the possibilities:

> . . . the best time to practice is in early childhood. Improvisation by young children, with adults keeping them safe, takes the form of 'pretend'—exploring the whole new world to see what it does and what I can do with it. And, with guidance, thinking intelligently about it—questioning, hypothesizing, problem-solving. (Jones 1996, p. 9)

Children also practice adult roles—as they play at cooking, going to work, or fixing and driving the car, they are practising being grown-up, consciously representing their future (Jones 1996) and using what they already know about these roles to build meaningful social knowledge.

Emotional development and play

As children engage in a variety of play activities, they have many opportunities to perceive themselves as competent, powerful and useful—as having something worthwhile to contribute to their world. These perceptions are vital to developing feelings of well-being and self-esteem, and are based on children's increasing skills and under-standing of their world. Building a block tower, digging a large hole, setting the table, dressing the baby and catching a big fish are all opportunities for children to develop their competence and sense of power and usefulness. Gradually, the tower gets taller, the hole bigger, and the table is set with more plates.

Some adults think that the best way to build children's self-esteem is to lavish attention on them and give them constant praise. In fact, this trivialises that very essence of the human spirit which is our inner self (Curry & Johnson 1989) and does little to help children see them-selves as competent, powerful and useful. As Katz says, 'lavishing praise for the mildest accomplishments' (Katz 1996, p. 12) is an unlikely strat-egy to strengthen children's self-esteem. Similarly, pre-packaged self-esteem kits with titles like 'I'm special' and 'Wonderful me' will also do little to strengthen children's self-esteem. They reduce self-esteem to something very personal, rather than recognising it as rooted in a community to which we all contribute, in which we should all be accepted and over which we should all have some power and control (Curry & Johnson 1989).

Some of our self-esteem comes from the way people respond to us. If people show us that they love us, despite our imperfections, and that we are accepted and belong, our feelings reflect this. However, much of our self-esteem comes from our own behaviour and com-petencies. It is not given by others, but comes from knowing that we can do certain things—it is a belief in ourselves, based on our com-petence (Evans 1995). Engaging in play allows children many oppor-tunities to do things for themselves, to practise them over and over again until they cry, 'look what I can do!' Children gain a sense of their own power and abilities—'look, I'm pouring mine, I'm making waves, I can swing myself!'—and their achievements—'look at my painting, look at my house, I built it all myself!'

When they engage in rich and meaningful play, children can exercise judgment, get to know and enjoy their power, and experience autonomy, mastery and competence. If they are unable to experience the power and satisfaction that comes in play, their emotional development is likely to be jeopardised (Levin 1996).

Cognitive development and play

Central to cognitive development is the capacity for symbolic thought, concept formation and understanding complex relationships. In play, children have almost unlimited opportunities to develop their symbolic capacities and to symbolise things using materials in ways that are interesting and meaningful to them. Dramatic play, block construction and painting and drawing are all examples of activities in which children are able to use either themselves or objects and materials to stand for something else: a block is a very fast police car, a doll is the baby, the child is the mother, the yellow lines are the flowers, the black dots are the rain. This symbolism is the precursor of later, more complex, symbolic activity including reading and writing, in which children recognise that lines and forms stand for speech, concepts and ideas.

In play, children have opportunities to further their conceptual understanding and their understanding of relationships like shape, size, space, numbers and measurement. When they play with objects they refine and extend their understanding of the quantitative qualities of objects—the size, shape and number of things—all of which are an essential part of mathematics. They learn, for instance, that four small blocks occupy the same space as one large one, or that two differently shaped containers hold the same amount—thus building new ideas onto what they already know and generalising their knowledge to apply to new and varied situations.

The skills which children learn to use as they play are, according to Levin, necessary prerequisites for later successful academic learning (Levin 1996). For instance, high quality play requires children to find content that is personally interesting to them to work on, containing new masteries to exercise, and new problems or questions to solve. As children persist in problem solving, they become creative thinkers, problem solvers and risk takers.

Physical development and play

Play that requires active use of the body gives children many opportunities to build their fine and gross motor control, enabling them gradually to gain more and more control over their bodies. Gross motor control is developed through activities that involve movements of the whole body or large parts of it, such as running, hopping, skipping, climbing, pushing, pulling and swinging. As children run, hop, skip and so on they use their existing gross motor skills to reach new levels of complexity, develop new skills and build their speed, endurance, balance and strength.

When children master a new skill, they enjoy it and practise it with glee, and it provides them with a wonderful sense of power and control. Children will often engage in the activity for long periods—walking along the beam balance over and over again, skipping everywhere or jumping from the deck repeatedly. Gradually, as they acquire prerequisite skills, they can master new skills that require complex coordination, such as riding a bicycle.

Fine motor control is developed through activities that involve the small muscles of the body and its extremities. As children pound clay, hammer in nails, draw patterns in the sand, cut with scissors and thread necklaces, their fine motor skills are refined and expanded with increasing dexterity and precision. Fine motor skills do not 'naturally' unfold—they are developed through exploration, experimentation and practice. That is, they are acquired as children actively engage with the world. As children play using fine motor skills they have already mastered, they encounter new challenges requiring new skills, which are in turn mastered through further play.

Conclusion

This chapter began by asking whether the current concerns about the devaluing and possible disappearance of play are justified. That play is disappearing is something about which current evidence is inconclusive. While there is little doubt that most young children spend many hours watching television and videos, we cannot assume that this activity displaces play. In fact, television may even facilitate play by providing children with a source of ideas for their play (Evans 1995). It also cannot be assumed that the hours spent watching television may have otherwise been spent playing; it may be that watching television is replacing other activities such as household chores (Evans

1995). Similarly, participation in organised sport does not necessarily mean that children engage less in self-initiated, self-organised game-playing; rather, it is more likely that the impact of organised sport is to change the nature of children's play rather than displace it. Evans (1995) suggests that children are playing different games (more associated with popular sports culture), in different places (less on the streets and backyards and more in parks and playgrounds), and in different ways (more rule-bound, as in organised sport).

Changing physical and social environments—for example, higher-density living, loss of back yard space, and restricted outdoor play as parents fear violence and other crimes against children—which on the surface may appear to inhibit children's play, are also more likely to change rather than displace it. Children adapt to their environment and find ways to play within it. Factor, who has studied the play of Australian children for 25 years, says:

> So powerful is the urge to play, to move outside the limitations of the immediate moment, the here and now, the status of small-ness, weakness, ignorance and powerlessness, that children even in the most terrible circumstances insist on playing. (Factor 1993, p. 22)

Clearly, we need much more research before we can conclude that children are playing less or that play is disappearing from children's daily lives. However, when we look in many of our early childhood classrooms, and when we talk with teachers and parents, there is undeniable evidence that many adults undervalue children's play. Increasing group sizes, expanded curricula (described by one early childhood educator as 'centimetres deep and kilometres wide'), limited session time requiring the adherence to rigid schedules, and the introduction of Basic Skills Testing in early childhood—all act as structural barriers to play.

Kagan (1996) suggests that lack of elaborate play in many American early childhood settings is often the result of attitudinal barriers. So too in Australia, where play is often accorded a lower status than work, and getting a good job is one of the most common goals in most people's lives. Many parents believe that the earlier their children's formal education begins, the better their chances for future achievement will be, and it seems likely that early formal education occurs at the expense of play (Evans 1995). Early childhood educators frequently report that they feel uncomfortable about including play in their classrooms because parents do not accept it as educationally valid. Many child care staff mention their discomfort when they are 'caught' either playing with children or sitting and observing their play. Families paying high fees expect that staff will be 'teaching' their children, not sitting in the sandpit with them or watching from the edge!

With both structural and attitudinal barriers militating against children's play, it does seem that there is cause for serious concern that play is being undervalued. If young children are denied opportunities to become deeply involved in play, develop the tools necessary for constructive play, and gain mastery and understandings through play, the implications for all aspects of their development and learning are serious (Levin 1996). They will be denied many opportunities to problem solve, put together ideas to create new meanings and develop symbolic capacities; nor will they be encouraged to practise being grown-up, exercise judgment, develop new and more complex physical skills and increase their strength, balance, speed, endurance and control.

For further thought and discussion

1. Do you think that children's play is disappearing—or changing?
2. Try to recall some of your own childhood play. What did you enjoy doing? Where did you play? Were adults involved? Did some play make you feel powerful, strong and in charge? Did you practise adult roles?
3. How would you respond to a group of parents who were concerned that their children were 'just playing?'
4. What strategies can early childhood educators use to break down attitudinal barriers to children's play?

References

Curry, N. & Johnson, C. 1989, *Beyond Self-Esteem: Developing a Genuine Sense of Human Value*, National Association for the Education of Young Children, Washington DC.

Elkind, D. 1981, *The Hurried Child*, Addison Wesley, Reading, Mass.

Elkind, D. 1987, *Miseducation: Preschoolers at Risk*, Knopf, New York.

Evans, J. 1995, 'Where have all the players gone?', *International Play Journal*, vol. 3, pp. 3–19

Factor, J. 1993, 'Enriching the play environment: creativity, culture and tradition', *Proceedings of the World Play Summit*, vol. 5, Melbourne, Australia.

Gordon, A. & Browne, K. 1993, *Beginnings and Beyond*, Delmar, New York.

Jones, E. 1996, 'Children's play: where dreams begin', *Pacific Oaks College Occasional Paper*, Pacific Oaks College, Pasadena.

Jones, E. & Reynolds, G. 1992, *The Play's the Thing: The Teacher's Roles in Children's Play*, Teachers College Press, New York.

Kagan, S. 1990, 'Children's play: the journey from theory to practice' in Klugman, E. and Smilansky, S. (eds) *Children's Play and Learning*, Teachers College Press, New York.

Katz, L. 1996, 'Are we confusing self-esteem with narcissism?' *DECSpress*, vol. 1(7), Aug., p. 12.

Levin, D. 1996, 'Endangered play, endangered development: a constructivist view of the role of play in development and learning' in Phillips A. (ed.) *Topics in Early Childhood Education 2: Playing for Keeps*, Inter-Institutional Early Childhood Consortium, Redleaf Press, St Paul, Minn.

Postman, N. 1982, *The Disappearance of Childhood*, Delacorte Press, New York.

Chapter 2

Stop, look and listen: adopting an investigative stance when children play

Elspeth Harley

> Play is a developmental activity through which human beings
> explore and discover their identity in relation to others through
> multiple media including their own bodies, projective media and
> a variety of role play. (Jennings 1995[a], p. 2)

Introduction

As early childhood educators we need to support children in learning how to engage in and enjoy play—in particular dramatic play and
role play. Children's involvement in such play allows them to benefit
from all the significant developmental outcomes that pretend play
offers (Shefatya 1995). It is through their role in dramatic play that
children learn to understand their everyday world and begin to draw
new meanings from it, using the opportunities, resources and materials that the family, culture, community and early childhood service
make available.

   In order to encourage children to develop as players, early childhood educators need to trust in children as players and develop the
patience and vision to look into their play rather than just at it. If we
look into a mirror we see an image, but it is only when we begin to
look into the image and question it that its full meaning emerges. To
the casual observer, children's play can appear, among many things,
fun, physical, unpredictable, serious, noisy and messy. However, when
early childhood educators adopt an investigative stance towards play
and become familiar with the criteria for assessing it, its full impact
becomes visible (Shefatya 1995). By observing, discussing, reading,
writing and telling stories of children's play we begin to understand
what it means for children and why every child needs to be a player.
This, in turn, brings new meaning and vitality to our practice and
work with children.

Play: a personal anecdote

Revisiting play takes me back nearly 30 years as I reflect on Andrew, a child I taught in my first year as a teacher. I was 20, Acting Director of a kindergarten and thought I knew a lot about play. My memory of our first meeting is vivid. 'I'm a horse!' he announced, and spent the rest of the day, and indeed weeks to come, being just that. He would gallop in each morning, neigh a greeting to the others and get on with the business of the day. This would include building a stable in the block corner, a farm in the sand area, being the passive horse, the hungry horse, the sick horse, the singing horse and numerous other characterisations of horses in his dramatic play.

How I longed for the horse and other children to sit quietly at the dough table or even paint! I offered tempting titbits, like rollers and cutters with the dough, even rainbow-coloured dough, but just when things would look like getting under control someone would burst into the room and announce, 'Come quickly, it's an emergency! Help! Everybody to the rescue—the horse is caught in quicksand, someone get a rope!' The dough table lost its attraction compared to the high drama being enacted outside.

The other children accepted the horse; I was the one who had the problem doing so. This creative, messy, unpredictable four-year-old posing as a horse was not something I had planned to have in my kindergarten. On reflection I believe I was insecure, not only because I didn't fully understand what was going on, but also because neither the player or the content was under my control.

I now believe that what Andrew did was enter the kindergarten in a role that was structured by him, at his pace for his particular purpose role—a role that helped him make sense of, and adapt to, this unfamiliar place called kindergarten. After a while Andrew stopped being the horse and his role playing and imagination took different paths. I remain grateful to this day that I didn't interfere and hijack his play. In 1966 I treated Andrew and his horse with indifference; today I would celebrate his joy, uniqueness and creativity.

Children's play is a very personal experience and purposeful activity. As early childhood educators observe, interpret and interact with children at play, we increase our understanding of the positive impact which play, and in particular dramatic play, can have on the development of the young child. Jennings (1993) maintains that children who are able to play will have more resources to draw on, both in childhood and in adult life. Dramatic play is therefore an important coping mechanism that allows children to process material that they do not understand and put it in a framework that makes sense to them. It can provide a playful space where life can be experimented with and choices explored.

Andrew's dramatic play provided such a framework—a safe place for him as well as a stimulating network of plans and ideas for other children. Children's dramatic play often puzzles us as adults, but to them it is a real and serious world, a place where they can create any identity and reveal very secret thoughts (Paley 1992).

Our observations in early childhood settings inform us that some children engage in dramatic play on a regular basis, others do so less frequently and some never at all. These variations raise some interesting questions about the differences between environments in the home and early childhood settings, players and non-players and the strategies used by early childhood educators to support both. If we believe that dramatic play is a coping mechanism for life, then what is our role as early childhood educators in facilitating children's dramatic play? Why are some children players and others not? Is it because non-players lack the skills and procedural knowledge about how to play, or because they lack the emotional skills and the ease needed to engage in dramatic play (Fein & Kinney 1994)?

In answering this we need to state that sadly, for many children, adults direct their play and the children are praised for reproducing what the adult wants. Such children are not allowed to develop their own imaginative and problem-solving resources and often become rigid players, afraid to take risks. Some children are comfortable when told what to do, but become uncomfortable when given a choice. Dramatic play which is about making choices can therefore become threatening to the child. Equally threatening can be an environment in which children receive no adult support or involvement in their play, where it becomes a random and aimless activity. These children may develop play that has no rules or boundaries, which can become frightening and out of control. For example, in some 'superhero play' a child may, in the role of 'superhero', carry out aggressive and violent acts.

If, as early childhood educators, we believe that all children should have relevant and meaningful play experiences, and that dramatic play is an essential part of their development, how can we give children the relevant knowledge and skills to become players? What strategies can we use?

The developmental paradigm of play

One strategy to ensure that children acquire the knowledge and skills necessary for meaningful play is to adopt the developmental paradigm of play evolved by Jennings (see Table 2.1). This can be used in early childhood settings for observation, assessment and planning for play, and has three stages: embodiment, projection and role. These stages develop in different ways but have a cumulative effect which is carried forward into more complex play activity. This progression is essential for dramatic play to develop fully in children.

This paradigm gives early childhood educators a tool for observing, assessing and evaluating children's play. It enables us to look into children's play as a prerequisite for planning and implementing strategies that will enable children to develop the relevant knowledge and skills to become players. In evaluating the paradigm we can understand its potential application in early childhood settings. It provides a framework that helps early childhood educators understand their role in supporting and extending children's play, and in particular role and dramatic play.

The following information on the paradigm and extracts about children at play vividly illustrate the applicability of the paradigm in early childhood settings.

Embodiment

The body is the primary means of learning for babies and infants. From the moment of birth, the young child receives experiences through the body in relation to other people and the environment.

Table 2.1: Developmental paradigm for use in observing the normal development of play in children aged 0–5 years (adapted from Jennings 1995(b), p. 134)

Embodiment:	Body and sensory play most prominent in the first year of life.
Projection:	Projective play, where experiences are projected out into various toys and media materials, such as sand and water, heighten the child's sensory experience. Toys take on roles and relationships, and the child controls the outcome.
Role:	Dramatic play where the child takes on the role of a character and moves into different roles. The child integrates the activity with the role and creates the story or directs the drama.

The child and adult are engaged in continual interaction and dialogue through the body. Nurturing and caring actions such as holding, feeding, rocking, washing, changing and dressing are crucial to the young child. The adult needs to be aware of the importance of increasing stimulating contact with the young child through different forms of touch, varying vocal sounds and talking. The child begins to interact and respond, imitating sounds and gestures. As the child learns to roll, sit, crawl and even walk, senses are being stimulated and in turn explored. The child's world begins to expand in the following ways:

- physical exploration of immediate surroundings;
- stimulation with a variety of sensations;
- being carried from place to place;
- increased mobility;
- increasing range of vocal sounds;
- awareness of other people. (Based on Jennings 1993, p. 27)

In relation to children's play and early childhood settings, it is important to recognise the early sensory play activity that starts before the child can walk. The child is able to make sounds in rhythm (banging an object on the floor or ground), moving to rhythm (jigging up and down on someone's lap), making marks (blowing bubbles, smearing food), and imitating sounds and facial expressions. Jennings defines this early activity as 'proto play' (Jennings 1993, p. 28).

How such play develops depends on the family, community and cultural influences surrounding the child. It is important to ensure that, in early childhood settings, opportunities are provided that allow children to explore, experiment and engage in activities and interactions that will nurture the development of their proto play. Activities to stimulate the senses—touch, taste, smell, sight and sound—should be available to children on a daily basis.

Georgia spends time in the company of her carer exploring a feely bag which contains a range of objects including a plastic spoon, a piece of velvet material, a wooden cat, a glass paperweight, a piece of fur, a ball of silver foil, a nail brush and an orange. The adult encourages her to explore each item, sharing new language and sensations with her.

Projection

In their early projective play children engage with water, sand, finger paint, clay, mud and a variety of other materials. For the child this is an important time of sensory stimulation and discovery. It is not a time when they should be directed or expected to make something.

> Theo enjoys the sensation of finger painting. He uses small circular motions with his index fingers in the paint and then with both hands he covers the table top with the paint. He experiments with different hand movements, moving the paint in different directions, making humming sounds as he pats and squishes his hands in the paint. When he has finished the adult helps him clean the table. There was no expectation that he would make a print or a picture. The focus has been on the experiencing and the doing.

As children develop an increasing aesthetic sense they will begin to explore the pattern, shape, colour and texture of different materials. This sensory and manipulative play develops fine motor and imaginative skills and allows them to represent their world in a symbolic way.

> Jack enjoys playing at the beach and spends time mixing sand and water in a bucket and making mounds with the wet sand. He digs and creates patterns with shells, seaweed and other items he has collected. Lizzie enjoys mixing earth and water, creating mud. She carefully arranges leaves, flowers, twigs and gum nuts in different patterns on her mud pats.

Both Jack and Lizzie are totally absorbed in their play. They find satisfaction in an experience over which they have control.

In later projective play, objects become toys and children project their ideas and feelings into different materials in their environment.

> Daisy, on finding a large rock, declares it to be her baby. 'My baby, my baby, where have you been?' Wrapping the rock in a blanket she carries it everywhere, talking to it, caressing, rocking, feeding it and putting it to sleep. Zac carries a red wooden block with him. He constantly makes ringing noises and uses it as a phone.

These children are creating experiences that are satisfying to them and are using objects in new and different ways. Through these experiences they are using their imagination and symbolic play as a way of processing their own experiences as well as creating some new possibilities.

Jane, an early childhood educator, shares an anecdote about a group of four-year-olds she works with. The children had seen media coverage of the funeral of the Princess of Wales. Using the dough, they made a large mound on the table and covered it with flowers and leaves they had collected from the centre garden. They asked Jane to write a sign for their creation: 'This is the island where Princess Diana is buried.'

In early childhood settings, we need to provide opportunities and time for children to explore and experiment with a range of sensory materials. Water play, where the child can develop sensory awareness and pleasure through splashing, pouring, bubble-making, and using different shaped containers, funnels and sponges, gives the child numerous opportunities to experiment with the feel, sensation and language of water. Sand and water play allow the child to experiment and make castles, rivers and dams. The addition of natural materials such as shells, pebbles, twigs and leaves allows the child to further experiment with shape, texture and pattern. Finger painting, working with clay, dough and a variety of collage materials as well as puppets, dolls, wooden or plastic animals, felt boards and felt characters are all important resources for early childhood settings. By not providing enough resources or time for these experiences we are denying children the opportunity to develop their sensory awareness and projective play. While the importance of these materials is well known to early childhood educators, we need to rethink the value of these materials in fostering children's imaginative and creative development and in supporting the development of their individual and social identity.

Role

It is during projective play with a variety of resources that children begin to take on the voice and gesture of others and expand their range of role playing. In the first stage, children enact their role playing through different projective materials including toys, puppets and dolls.

James is playing with a collection of wooden people and animals figures that he is arranging in a doll's house. Picking up the dog shape he makes barking noises as he crashes the dog in and out of different rooms of the house. Picking up the mother shape, he changes his voice to a higher pitch, screaming at the dog, 'Get out of this house now, get to your kennel!' As he removes the dog to a corner, he begins to make crying noises and picks up the baby figure, whispering, 'Shh, shh, the naughty dog has gone.'

As their play develops and becomes more complex, children take on dramatic roles instead of projecting them through toys and other objects. They act out roles from their family and community or from stories and television. Their role playing begins to include dressing up, making props and developing an environment or special space for their play. As children act out events and stories they start including others in their game. They improvise scenes and characters and take on real and imagined roles.

Maddie, Ben and Joseph have built a 'secret and magic cave' under a large tree with rugs and old blankets. They use several old pots to mix a magic potion made from 'water, leaves, rose petals, invisible stinging nettles and gold', and chant a magic spell, 'abracadabra, hocus pocus, lizzie, dizzie, one fried goanna, two dead mice, *zoom!*' In their play Maddie and Ben are cave creatures and Joseph is their pet dinosaur. When they drink the magic potion, Maddie and Ben became space creatures who are looking for a pet dinosaur to take back to the moon. Lydia and Fee join in the play and are instructed by Maddie to be the baby-sitters for the pet dinosaur. Lambros and Charlie are in the sandpit making pizzas and join the game with moon pizzas for everyone. The game continues, elaborated in different ways over several days.

The role of the early childhood educator

In the earlier stages of embodiment and projection of play, the early childhood educator's role is to provide appropriate materials and experiences in which children can engage and interact. Early childhood educators need to act as mediators, supporting children's interactions with materials as well as with other children. For children engaging in dramatic role play, early childhood educators may need to intervene in a variety of ways, including taking on the role of co-player and actively participating in children's dramatic play. This participation can include modelling roles and offering ideas and knowledge to enhance the play and support the child's growth (Jones & Reynolds 1992).

In their dramatic play, as the extracts show, children are able to create their world in new and different ways. Children's capacity to role play enables them to understand themselves and others better. It is through their dramatic play that children continue to develop both their individual and social identity. It is important in early childhood settings that educators provide not only the time, space and props for dramatic play but also provide a range of role models with whom children can identify (Singer & Singer 1991). Many children have a range of television role models but often lack live social models from their culture or community.

Pauline, an early childhood educator, introduces the children in her centre to different members in the community responsible for the collection and recycling of rubbish. The children meet the local council gardener who speaks about her role in keeping the local parks clean, and are able to observe the collection of household garbage and speak to the driver of the recycling truck. Later in their play these children use the outdoor blocks to construct a sophisticated recycling truck and create the various compartments for the different categories of recyclable material. They role play a range of council workers and inspectors responsible for collecting and sorting the rubbish.

Children's capacity to play and dramatise will be influenced by their family, community, culture and learning experiences. Early childhood settings therefore have a crucial role in children's play through the provision of a program that promotes and values play for all children. The developmental paradigm provides a very useful tool for early childhood educators to use. If, as educators, we are able to assess and evaluate children's play, we can make play possible and help children to get better at it (Jones & Reynolds 1992).

Jesse is four years old and attends a preschool group. He has had difficulty settling into the group and spends a lot of time alone, observing his peers at play, but not interacting with them.

Terri and Mark, the early childhood educators working with the group, identify Jesse's need for a lot more sensory experiences to support the development of his proto play and early projective play. They plan an individual program that includes supporting and extending his sensory play. They provide a variety of sensory activities, including feely bags, texture boxes, water play, bubbles, finger paint and simple movement to music which are suitable both on his own and with a partner. Jesse needs initial one-to-one support to engage in these activities, but as his confidence grows he is able to work alongside other children, beginning to initiate activities for himself.

The capacity to play exists in all children and we should never assume that because a child has a disability that child is unable to develop their play skills and use their imagination (Singer & Singer 1991).

Mary has cerebral palsy and attends an early childhood centre, depending on the use of a frame to support her mobility. She spends a lot of time watching and observing her peers. One morning at the centre the children discovered a piece of sparkling quartz in the sandpit. The cry went up, 'Treasure, treasure, there's treasure in the sandpit!' This simple discovery led to a rich and engaging play experience for many of the children, including Mary. A treasure ship was constructed with a magic control panel that enabled children to go anywhere in the universe to hunt for treasure.

Over a period of days, more treasure was discovered—in Africa, in a rainforest and in a castle. Treasure was buried and treasure maps were made. Mary would stand, supported by her frame, observing the purposeful activity her peers were engaged in. A plank was constructed on the treasure ship leading to the magic control panel. Mary came closer to the play and, after observing it for a while, indicated that she too would like a turn on the magic control panel. This was the first time Mary had initiated any interaction with her peers. Without hesitation her peers responded to her request, and set about solving how to get Mary onto the treasure ship and support her as she walked up the plank to the control panel. It took a lot of time and problem-solving techniques, but finally they made it happen! With a peer on each arm and an adult supporting her back Mary was able to walk up the plank, not just once but over and over to the delight of her peers, educators and, later that day, her mother. Mary became part of the continuing play, engaging with her peers and dressing up for the first time.

Dramatic play not only gave Mary a role to play, but enhanced her individual identity, as well as giving her a social and group identity. Dramatic play has a great deal of inclusive potential and it is important that educators highlight its positive role in children's development. If, as educators, we can value and share children's play, we will be able to increase the status of play as well as the self-esteem of the players.

Conclusion

As the title of this chapter suggests, early childhood educators have a responsibility to look at the primary importance of play in children's development and ensure that all children in their centre or care have access to role and dramatic play. However, access alone is not enough. Educators need to stop, look and listen in order to determine what knowledge, skills and support individual children need in order to engage in role and dramatic play. As early childhood educators, we all need the patience and vision to look *into* children's play, not just *at* it. Our observations provide the tool to allow us to support play and intervene in it in planned and imaginative ways. Play starts at birth, and early childhood environments that promote play for all children and allow all children to feel motivated, esteemed and appreciated are cause for celebration.

For further thought and discussion

1. What equipment and resources do you have available in your centre to support the development of children's projective play? What time and space do you allow for children to develop their projective play?
2. What opportunities do you provide in your centre for children to engage in sensory play?
3. To what extent do children in your centre engage in role and dramatic play? Which children are players, and which are non-players? What evidence do you have for this? What strategies do you use to support players and non-players alike in your centre?

References

Fein, G. & Kinney, P. 1994, 'He's a nice alligator: observations on the affective organisation of pretence', in *Children at Play: Clinical and Developmental Approaches to*

Meaning and Representation, Slade, A. & Palmer Wolfe, D., (eds), Oxford University Press, Oxford.

Jennings, S. 1993, *Playtherapy with Children: A Practitioner's Guide*, Blackwells Scientific, Oxford.

Jennings, S. 1995(a), *Theatre Ritual and Transformation: The Senoi Temiars*, Routledge, London.

Jennings, S. 1995(b), 'Playing for real', *International Play Journal*, vol. 3.

Jones, E. & Reynolds, G. 1992, *The Play's the Thing: Teachers' Roles in Children's Play*, Teachers College Press, New York.

Paley, V. 1992, *You Can't Say You Can't Play*, Harvard University Press, Cambridge, MA.

Shefatya, L. 1995, 'The assessment of dramatic and sociodramatic play: goals, tools, criteria and conceptual frameworks', in *Play, Policy and Practice*, Klugman, E. (ed.), Redleaf Press, St Paul, Minnesota.

Singer, D. & Singer, J. 1991, *The House of Make Believe: Children's Play and the Developing Imagination*, Harvard University Press, Cambridge, MA.

Chapter 3

Thinking about play, playing about thinking

Sue Dockett

Main Editor's note

The Barbara Creaser Memorial Lecture Fund was established in 1995 following Barb's untimely death at the age of 55, to acknowledge the great contribution she made to the early childhood field. Part of that contribution related to her passion for socio-dramatic play and her messages about how important it is. Children all over Australia and overseas have benefited, and continue to do so, from those messages through her publications on play.

It was determined by the Board responsible for the Barbara Creaser Memorial Lecture series that the inaugural lecture would be given by an Australian on the topic of play. Dr Sue Dockett was selected as the inaugural presenter of the lecture, presented in 1996, the content of which follows in this chapter.

The Barbara Creaser Memorial Lecture Fund Board acknowledges with gratitude this contribution made by Dr Dockett.

Introduction

When writing this paper, I managed to get myself tied up into a number of knots: what exactly did I want to say that was innovative and exciting, and how did that relate to the extensive body of research that underpins play? I wanted to be critical but creative, yet acknowledge the wealth of research that has already occurred in the area of play. Much of this research has been conducted in Australia, yet we still appear to rely predominantly on American and British research. People like Barb Creaser contributed a great deal to our understanding about play and to the promotion of pretend play within early childhood settings, yet we tend to value overseas research more readily than the contribution that has come to us from our own colleagues.

In the midst of my deliberations, I was lucky enough to have a conversation about a range of irrelevant things with one of my colleagues, Sue Farmer, who asked me, 'do you want to renovate or restore?' As early childhood educators, we decided that this question was most applicable to what I was trying to do in this paper and we played around with it for a while. Did I want to update existing views of play, building on the foundation we already had, or did I want to go back to and restore the original work of, for instance, Piaget, Vygotsky and Parten and remind educators of its applicability and importance?

After reviewing a range of literature, conducting my own research and talking with a number of people, I think I can say that I'm here to renovate! If we look closely, there are termites in the rafters of our conventional views about play and, while some serious restoration is required to ensure that the basic foundation remains intact, we can use new timber and new methods to build a solid structure around it.

To begin this process of renovation, we need to consider the foundations, then focus on what is crumbling around us and needs to be replaced. The foundations include:

- how we define play;
- the notion that children engage in different types of play;
- play as a cognitive as well as a social experience;
- the ability of adults to observe and interpret children's play.

The structures that appear to be under threat of falling in include:

- the frameworks we use when observing and interpreting play;
- the focus on a developmental sequence of play behaviours;
- what happens during play.

An example of play will help set the context for this discussion.

Wombat Stew

A group of four-year-olds have just heard the story of 'Wombat Stew'. It is a story they have read before and they ask for it to be read again. As they move outside, they start collecting things to make their own Wombat Stew. Several large tubs and buckets have been especially provided.

Chris is stirring a pot of sand and dirt.

Lauren (adding more sand): This makes kangaroos.

Karen: Got chocolate. (adds dirt)

Simon: Got lottsa chocolate to make it yummier! That's what you have in wombat stew.

Chris: After the dingo tastes it . . . he will run away. An' then he won't see the wombat for ever an' ever!

Simon (mixing): Yeah!

Chris: I got some sticks in there. An' feathers.

Simon: An' chocolate. I'm the wombat. I'm not the one that goes in the stew. I'm the wombat who sings Wombat Stew!

(Emily and Belinda join in)

Chris: No more grass. He tasted it!

Simon (picking up some in his fingers): This is the nice part. (pretends to eat it)

Chris (shouting): Nearly finished!

Emily: I can watch!

Louise: What are you doing?

Simon: We're making Wombat Stewwwwwww!

Louise: Are they cooking wombats?

Chris and Simon: No! Wombat Stew.

Simon: It's just got bugs an' everything in it.

Chris: It's finished. Eat it!

Matthew: Now we eat it . . . yummy, yummy, yummy!

The play was halted by lunch. After lunch, Simon began making more Wombat Stew. He took the big bowl and filled it with sand, dirt, leaves and the like.

Simon is joined by Lachlan. Simon has a large bowl and is filling it with sand as he stirs.

Simon: Let's make Wombat Stew again!

Lachlan: Yeah! (to Ben) We makin' Wombat Stew! Get some more grass. We mix . . . need some sticks and some sand.

Simon: Here's sticks. Chewy chewy Wombat Stew!

Lachlan: Now we're puttin' googy eggs in it! (stirs with stick)

Simon: 'Cause we're bad for Wombat Stew!

Lachlan: We're witches! (still stirring) No, not a witch . . . hasn't got a hat on.

Simon: Yeah . . . black pointy hat! (makes shape of hat on head with hands)

Lachlan: I'm looking at it. Dirty eggs. (drops dirt in and stirs)

Simon: Pretend this is chewing gum in it. (adds play dough in small pieces to the 'stew')

Lachlan: Burn your fingers! Very hot!

Simon: Any barks? (gets up to look for bark to go in the stew)

(Lauren adds some gumnuts)

Simon: We're witches!

They all leave the pot and run off as witches.

Defining play

When I was observing the Wombat Stew episode, I recognised very quickly that it was play. There were certain words and actions that identified it as such but, as much as anything, it was the mode of interaction that signalled what the children were doing (Bruner 1977). However, the interaction also contained features that have been described as the defining attributes of play. While there are several ways in which we can define play, the attributes identified by Sponseller (1982) are particularly relevant:

- internal motivation;
- internal control;
- internal reality.

For example, the children engaged in the play because they chose to, rather than because it had been suggested to them. It was a story they had requested be read and, with the help of the props supplied by the adults, one that they enacted in various ways. Control rested with the children (some had greater levels of control than others) and there was no direct adult intervention in the play, which continued for over 40 minutes in the morning and was revisited by some of the players during the afternoon, albeit briefly.

Evidence that the children were creating their own internal reality occurred throughout the play, especially when they indicated that they were pretending to eat the stew. When the play resumed after lunch, there were clear statements about pretending and reality; for example, Simon pretended that the dough in the stew was chewing-gum. As the play moved from the Wombat Stew theme to a witch theme, the pretence is made obvious to all the players through both words and actions.

Observing and interpreting play

What information can be gleaned from our observation and interpretation of such play? One way of interpreting it is to consider the cognitive stages of play outlined by Piaget (1945) and later by Smilansky (1968); that is, functional play, constructive play, dramatic play and games with rules. In the Wombat Stew example, there is evidence of functional play, as Chris stirs the pot of sand and assorted ingredients. There is also evidence of constructive play, in that the children are working towards creating or constructing an entity—the stew. There is a great deal of evidence of dramatic play, as the children use materials to represent the ingredients of the stew and as they use a range of objects 'as if' they were something else. There is not a lot of evidence of games with rules, although there do seem to be implicit rules about who has the controlling interest and the roles of the respective players. In summary, we can identify a predominance of dramatic play and note the level of involvement of a range of children in this type of play.

Another way we could consider this episode is to relate it to Parten's (1932) social categories of play. In this way, we can identify some onlooker behaviour from Emily, and associative and cooperative play at various times between Matthew, Chris and Simon. There is no evidence of unoccupied, solitary or parallel play.

Combining the Piaget/Smilansky categories with Parten's social categories in a matrix results in a framework which can be used to observe and interpret play (see Table 3.1). This provides useful information about the types of play in which children engage and enabled me, in some of my investigations, to focus on examples of cooperative dramatic play (Docket 1994).

Play as a cognitive and social experience

Combining the cognitive and social categories of play emphasises the interrelation of cognitive and social factors in much of children's play. This is something that features in the theories of Piaget and Vygotsky. The Piagetian position emphasises that play is both a driving force for development and a mirror for development that has already occurred; the Vygotskian position is that play is a leading source of

Table 3.1: Matrix combining the Piaget/Smilansky and Parten categories of play

	Social categories					
Cognitive categories	Unoccupied	Onlooker	Solitary	Parallel	Associative	Cooperative
Functional						
Constructive						
Dramatic						
Games with rules						

both cognitive and effective development (Rusher, Cross & Ware 1995). In keeping with the Piagetian view and Parten's categories, we expect children to engage in a developmental progression of play behaviours, moving from the simple to the complex—that is, from the simple manipulation of objects to the application of complex pretend play scenarios and scripts, and from uninvolved or solitary play to that which involves others in a complex, cooperative interaction. These sequences may be identified in much of children's play and they can be used to provide a range of information about children's cognitive and social development.

However, there are also drawbacks to using this sort of categorisation. How, for instance, does it enable us to take into account the fact that more than one type or combination of play often occurs simultaneously within the same episode? The Wombat Stew example is part of an overall episode that lasted for almost an hour, and during that time the players were engaged in several different types of play; for example, at different times Chris was engaging in functional, constructive and symbolic play.

How should we code such an episode? One strategy might be to code the most 'advanced' type of play observed—that is, the dramatic/cooperative combination. Is this typical of the episode? Another strategy might be to sample the play every five minutes or so for a period of 10–15 seconds and to code the play observed for individual children during this time—but again, we need to ask, how typical of the episode is that sampling? Coding an episode in one way only may not result in an accurate portrayal of the play (Takhvar & Smith 1990).

Another problem arises when we observe play that doesn't fit the categories. In the next example, two five-year-old boys, Sasha and Brad, engage in some fascinating play with words. Yet this sort of play doesn't feature in the cognitive and social categories described.

A cut-mermaid

Sasha and Ben are sitting in the sandpit, sprinkling sand around from a plate piled high with sand. Their feet are in the sand.
Sasha: This is poisonous. Poisonous chook stuff.
Brad: It's poison one. You just feed it to the chooks.
Sasha: Now let's feed the chooks now.

Brad and Sasha: Here chook chook chook chook, chook, chook.
Sasha: Only chooks.
Brad: My chooks are over here.
Sasha: Here chook, chook, chook! (to imaginary chooks) This is bread. Here chook, chook, chook.
Brad: Here cow, cow, cow, cow! (laughs)
Sasha: Here horse, horse, horse, horse, horse, horse, horse, horse, horse! (more laughter)
Brad: Here farm, farm, farm.
Sasha: Here farmhouse, farmhouse, farmhouse.
Brad: Here farm, um, here, farmhouse, farmhouse, farmhouse.
Sasha: Here farmhouse, farmhouse, farmhouse.
Brad: This farmhouse! (laughs)
Sasha: Hey, there's sharks in there. (points to the sandpit) Nothing left. No more sharks.
Brad: Just fishes. No, they're bitey fishes. Can put your feet back in when there's no fishes. Should put 'em in now! Hey, hey, hey! There's a biting whale in here!
Sasha: Whale, whale, here whale, whale. Here whale, whale, whale. Here, whale, whale, whale . . .
Brad: The whale said 'Nothing in it'. 'Tend you are a swordfish. They cut with their noses.
Sasha: They cut. (brings both arms together and opens and closes them) I'm a sword-mermaid! (laughs) A cut-mermaid. Cut, cut, cut.
Brad: We haven't got any feet.
Sasha: We're just mermaids with our tails.
Brad: They swim with their tails.

This episode of play, lasting about 15 minutes, is quite complex. It involves elements of pretend play and interaction between the two players, but where does it fit into the matrix in Table 3.1? It could be cooperative play and it could be dramatic play, but the essence of the play is lost if it is categorised either way. We need a more flexible method of analysis.

The same criticism applies to rough-and-tumble play. We might be able to fit it into one of the categories of play, but doing so reduces its importance and value. Rough-and-tumble play can involve complex interaction, yet it doesn't really belong in the Piaget/ Smilansky and Parten classification. We could probably fit it into Table 3.1, but this would be unlikely to result in a realistic view of the nature of children's play interactions.

A further danger is that we tend to use the cognitive/social categories as a reflection of a developmental stage. In many circumstances, this may be an accurate reflection of children's developing abilities and understandings. However, it is also possible that it does not accurately reflect them at all. In a discussion of some of the limitations of viewing play in terms of the Piaget/Smilansky and Parten categories, Reifel and Yeatman argue that by 'expecting to see a particular set of developmental steps in a particular order, we are biasing our observations and judgements about children's behaviour. By associating a certain type of play with a certain age or stage, we may also miss that different types of play may relate to one another' (Reifel & Yeatman 1993, p. 351).

Expecting to see particular stages of play development has the added disadvantage of interpreting the play behaviours of Western middle-class children as the 'norm' and describing variations from this as deficits (Göncü & Tuermer 1995). I've yet to read a variation of this sort described as 'advanced'. The Western middle-class norm approach pays little heed to cultural and social differences among groups. Göncü and Tuermer (1995) call for a greater emphasis on observing play, and developing categories for that play, from what we see rather than putting children's play into predetermined categories.

Alternative views of play

If we accept these criticisms, what are some alternative frameworks we can use for analysing children's play? Let us look at some that have been suggested.

Play styles

One approach to play is that outlined by Creaser (1990) who details three different play styles. Rather than looking at the category of play in which children engage, she focuses on the children involved in play and highlights their preferred ways of approaching situations. In her description of explorers, spectators and dramatists, Creaser investigates children's preferred ways of interacting, and how adults can enhance children's play through an awareness of these styles. While the master dramatist in Creaser's description demonstrates a facility with pretence that may be reflected in the Piaget/Smilansky and Parten categories, the focus on the child as a player reminds us that it is the children and their interpretation of what is happening that is important, rather than adult perspectives of what may or may not be happening.

Play and mental representation

Another way of describing play is to consider it as an indication of children's ability to use mental representation. While this is particularly relevant to dramatic play, even functional play can involve a level of mental representation as a child seeks to imitate an action seen previously.

In dramatic play—often referred to as pretend play, in this context—objects are used 'as if' they were something else (Fein 1987). In other words, they are used to *represent* something and it is the players themselves who determine what form this representation will take. Of particular interest is that children as young as two years old can quite readily distinguish reality (they have a block in their hand) from the pretence (the block is being used as if it were a car). The significance of this, according to Leslie (1987) is that these children must have two mental representations of which they are aware and between which they can move during their interaction.

This has been taken to indicate that young children develop a theory of mind (Dockett 1996; Lillard 1993). This is essentially a recognition that, as humans, our minds interpret the information we receive from our environment. Astington describes a theory of mind as an awareness 'children have of their own minds and others' minds and of the relation between the mind and the world. This understanding enables children to predict and explain actions by ascribing mental states, such as beliefs, desires and intentions, to themselves and to other people' (Astington 1991, p. 158).

One of the essential features of a theory of mind is the ability to distinguish between pretence and reality. In her description of what constitutes pretence, Lillard (1993) uses the metaphor developed by Austin that pretence involves 'stretching one "reality" over another, or holding "one thing in front of another in order to protect or conceal or disguise it"' (Austin 1979, p. 260). Hence, the underlying feature of pretence is that it is contrasted with reality and that the pretend and the real situations are not confused. As a result, when they engage in pretence, children are consistently able to separate pretence from reality. Conversely, pretence must involve actions or events that are not the same as reality. This means that children cannot pretend to be themselves as they really are at that moment—Jason can pretend to be asleep, for instance, only if he is really not asleep. Lillard refers to this as a paradox and notes that:

If I am trying to eat a block because I believe it's a cookie, then I am not pretending; rather, I am mistaken. On the other hand, if I enact the same eating behaviour knowing full well that what I am acting on is in fact a block, then I am pretending. To be truly pretending, one must grasp the situation on two levels; both as the real situation (the block) and as the pretend situation (the cookie). (Lillard 1993, p. 350)

Considered in this way, pretence becomes a complex activity. This does not mean that children understand it completely; rather that using pretence is something they do with relative ease. If we consider play in terms of children's use of mental representation, we can describe a pattern of complexity which ranges from imitating acts—with or without other people involved—to pretending and involving others in a complicated and sustained pattern of pretence (Dockett 1994, 1995). In the Wombat Stew example, some children indicated clearly in both words and action that they were pretending. While this is a positive approach not dissimilar to that of Piaget, what is missing is the focus on stages of cognitive and social development.

Children's play can contain a number of implicit and explicit indications that they are not only able to pretend, but are also able to understand that others pretend and can adjust their own actions to take into account the perspectives of others. Children's conversation can demonstrate this, as indicated in the following example.

Family matters

Ben and Simon, late in the same afternoon they made Wombat Stew, are digging in the sandpit.

Ben: Let's play Mums and Dads. Simon, you can be the dog.

Simon: The cat?

Ben: No, the dog.

Simon: The sister dog?

Ben: I'm the Dad, and you be the dog.

Simon (gets on to all fours and move across the sand): Pretend you have a cat too.

Ben: Here's the dog food. (places a plate of sand in front of Simon)

Simon: Woof, woof! (puts mouth to sand, pretends to eat sand)

Ben: Don't eat it, don't eat it! Just pretend!

Simon: This was Wombat Stew, now it's changed to dog food!

(Dockett 1993)

Play—moving towards intersubjectivity

Closely linked with the emphasis on play as mental representation is what could be described as a move towards intersubjectivity. During the early childhood years, one of the observable patterns of play inter-action relates to children's increasing ability to take account of the perspectives of others and to predict and explain their actions, based on a shared understanding of the situation. This does not mean, however, that children do it all the time; that they are always successful in this area; or that the failure to use these understandings successfully is a developmental concern.

Both Piagetian and Vygotskian descriptions of play highlight the importance of becoming aware of the perspectives of others, albeit for different reasons (Dockett & Perry 1996). Piaget (1965) stresses the importance of children interacting and cooperating with their peers as a means of becoming aware of different perspectives, adopting roles, and creating and resolving cognitive conflicts (Perret-Clermont & Brossard, 1985). Cognitive conflict occurs when partners in a task have different points of view and the skills necessary to share them. The focus, however, remains on the individual child's changing under-standing of the world as a result of this interaction or conflict.

The Vygotskian view concentrates instead on the value of social interaction between the more skilled members of a social group. Such interaction occurs within the zone of proximal development and is underpinned by intersubjectivity. Intersubjectivity is described by Canella as 'the process of constructing and reconstructing joint purposes between the child and his/her interacting partner' (Canella 1993, p. 429). What does this mean? For Canella, it involves these steps:

- each player coming to the situation with his/her own perspective;
- deciding on common reference points (for example, players agree-ing on a particular task or direction) through communication medi-ated by the players;
- each player adapting to the others;
- players sharing purpose and meaning that they would not have created alone.

In following these steps, children develop what Göncü describes as a 'joint understanding between players' (Göncü 1993, p. 99). Rather than moving through an invariant set of stages of play, this understanding focuses on the interaction within play and the children's developing intersubjectivity.

Göncü (1993) describes the increasingly intersubjective nature of children's play as being evident in their dialogue during play and in their ability to expand the play interaction by contributing new ideas or materials at appropriate times, expressing agreement and emphasising their own ideas. Older children are described as extending play by building onto it or adding new dimensions. One of the important considerations here is the awareness children must have of others to be able to do this successfully. In order to build upon a play theme, children need to understand what is happening in the play, what roles are being played and their relevance, as well as being aware of what is likely to be accepted by the other players. In other words, they need to be aware of what the others are thinking and be able to anticipate their words and actions. In this respect, developing intersubjectivity—that is, a shared focus of interaction—and an increasing awareness of mental representations have much in common.

The following example highlights both the shared focus of interaction and an awareness of the mental states of others, as players discuss, allocate and explain the roles.

Dads and dogs

Jess, Jade, Mathew, Sally and Dale (all aged four to five) are in the kitchen area of the preschool.

Jess: Tonight we cooking this (holds up gravy packet) and this (holds up chocolate dog biscuit packet).

Sally: Oh yuk!

Jess (laughing): I'm gonna cook some dog biscuits!

Sally (on all fours with her tongue out, pretending to be a dog): It's a dog!

Jess: You gotta eat all the dog food! (places plate on the floor near Sally) Dog, that's your dinner, all right? For tonight! (turns to table, sees empty box of chocolates, opens booklet explaining the sorts of chocolates which used to be in the box. Pretends to pick up a chocolate and place it in her mouth) Yum! I think I'll put these in the little girl cupboard.

Jade: I'm sorry! I'm sorry, I'm the mum. I'm sorry, I'm the mum. (Jess turns around and stands facing Jade, hands on hips) An' you be the Mum. The other Mum.

Mathew: What can I be?

> *Sally*: You can be the sister. No, the Dad.
> *Jess*: No, I'll be the Dad.
> *Dale*: You need a boy for a Dad. Didn't they tell you that?
> *Jess*: Well, I'm the Daddy too.
> *Dale*: No.
> *Jess*: I'm the Dad. I'm the good Dad.
> *Sally* (to Dale): You're the Dad.
> *Jade* (to Jess): You be the grandfather.

An important feature of an analysis of play in terms of mental representation or intersubjectivity is a focus on what is happening during play interactions. That is, it is not considered sufficient to describe the type of play or even to assume that children in the same area doing the same thing are playing; instead, it is seen as necessary to focus on exactly what is happening during the play interaction.

This approach has some distinct advantages in that it does not presume a clear progression though a series of stages of play and it has the potential to lead us to a greater knowledge of individual differences and preferences. It should also mean that, as adults, we can be more responsive to the needs of children at play and create far more challenging play environments.

However, there is also the danger that, as we move away from more global assessments of play—such as the Piaget/Smilansky and Parten categorisation—to focus on specific features and elements of play, we start to lose sight of the wider picture. We need to remind ourselves not to lose sight of the essence of play, and that the phenomenon of play may well be more than the sum of its parts.

Playing with thinking

Our discussion so far has focused on how we, as adults, think about play and how we can identify increasing intersubjectivity and developing theories of mind in children's play. Are these matters important to children? Or are we adults making children's play much more complicated than it really is?

In some of my observations it has been clear that children are aware of their own beliefs, desires and intentions, as well as those of other children, and that their interaction is based on such an awareness. In some instances, children demonstrate the ability to play with thinking.

In the following example, Max appears to be making fun of Harvey's speech pattern (he uses 'me' instead of 'I'), and Harvey realises that Max is upset when he tells him that he is not going to be his friend. Harvey understands the desire of Max to be friends and uses the knowledge that unfulfilled desires lead to being upset to exploit this situation with Max.

You are not my friend

Max (aged four and a half) has recently arrived at preschool. Harvey (aged almost five) arrives and runs over to Max.

Harvey: Me back!

Max (in imitative voice): Me back!

Harvey (looks at Max): You not my friend!

Max: I am your friend. You'll be my friend the next day, I know.

Harvey: Me not be your friend next day!

Max: Why?

Harvey: 'Cause.

Max: Why?

Harvey: Just 'cause!

Max: Are you Malcolm's friend?

Harvey: Na.

Max: Are you Robert's friend?

Harvey: Na. Me not your friend neither. No one's friend.

Max: No one's friend? Why? Any friend?

Harvey: 'Cause I hate you!

Max (approaching Malcolm): Malcolm, are you my friend? Harvey's not your friend. Are you my friend? (follows Malcolm around the room asking if he is his friend)

(Dockett 1994)

In another instance, Caitlin (aged four) explained how she 'had an idea in her mind', but then 'lost it in her thinking', cause it 'just went out of her head', but if she thought about it hard enough, it might just 'pop back into her mind'. From a colleague comes the example of her four-year-old son who noticed a safety pin in the car. He said, 'mum, I know why you've got that safety pin there'. 'Why?' his mother asked. 'So you don't have an accident,' he replied.

Just as children play with concrete objects, so they play with language, ideas and thinking. Part of our task as early childhood educators is to listen to children as they play and to value that play for what it is, as well as to ensure that we provide as many opportunities as possible for children to build upon and extend both their playing and their understanding.

Conclusion

There is a rich and varied history of research on children's play. In seeking to renovate, rather than restore, my task has been to try to identify the foundations of our approaches to studying play and to ensure that these remain strong. In addition, we have the responsibility to question what we do, and how and why we do it. Where our actions serve to prop up a structure which no longer seems viable, we need to seek alternative structures. It is in this vein that I propose some different ways of thinking about play and recognising the 'playing with thinking' in which children engage.

Barb Creaser prompted this train of thoughts when she focused on the players and their styles of interactions, rather than seeking only to categorise children's play. Her work reminds us that it is the *player* who makes the play—not our observation or interpretation of the event. It's a message that needs to be reinforced as we look for ways in which we, as adults, seek to understand children's play while at the same time realising that, because play is owned and controlled by the players, we will often be only onlookers.

For further thought and discussion

1. What evidence do you see in young children's play that they understand the perspectives or intentions of others?
2. After observing a small group of children at play, consider any steps taken to establish intersubjectivity. What strategies were used? Which were successful?
3. Do young children realise that they are pretending in play? How do you know?
4. What does children's speech indicate about their knowledge of other children's thinking and actions?

References

Astington, J. 1991, 'Intention in the child's theory of mind', in *Children's Theories of Mind: Mental States and Social Understanding*, Frye D. & Moore C. (eds), Erlbaum Hillsdale, NJ.

Austin, J. 1979, 'Pretending', in *Philosophical Papers*, Urmson J. & Warnock G. (eds), Oxford University Press, Oxford.

Bruner, J. 1977, 'Introduction', in Tizard B. & Harvey D. (eds), *The Biology of Play*, Spastics International Medical Publications, London.

Canella, G. 1993, 'Learning through social interaction: shared cognitive experience, negotiation strategies, and joint concept construction for young children', *Early Childhood Research Quarterly*, vol. 8, pp. 427–44.

Creaser, B. 1990, *Pretend Play: A Natural Path To Learning*, Australian Early Childhood Resource Booklet No. 5, Australian Early Childhood Association, Canberra.

Dockett, S. 1993, 'When planning for play isn't enough', *Paper presented at the Fifth Australia and New Zealand Conference on the First Years of School*, Perth.

Dockett, S. 1994, Young children's developing theories of mind, unpublished Ph.D. thesis, University of Sydney.

Dockett, S. 1995, *'I tend to be dead and you make me alive': Developing Understandings through Sociodramatic Play*, Australian Early Childhood Resource Booklet No. 3, Australian Early Childhood Association, Canberra.

Dockett, S. 1996, 'Children as theorists', in *DAPcentrism: Challenging Developmentally Appropriate Practice*, Fleer, M. (ed.), Australian Early Childhood Association, Canberra.

Dockett, S. & Perry, B. 1996, 'Re: playing (and) constructivism', *Proceedings of the Sixth Australia and New Zealand Conference on the First Years of School*, Hobart, Jan.

Fein, G. 1987, 'Pretend play: creativity and consciousness', in Gorlitz, D. & Wohlwill J. (eds), *Curiosity, Imagination and Play: On the Development of Spontaneous Cognitive and Motivational Processes*, Erlbaum Hillsdale, NJ.

Göncü, A. 1993, 'Development of intersubjectivity in the dyadic play of preschoolers', *Early Childhood Research Quarterly*, vol. 8, pp. 99–116.

Göncü, A. & Tuermer, U. 1995, Pretend play in a low-income African–American community, in Göncü A. & Nicolopoulou A. (chairs), 'The pretend play of cultures; cultures of pretend play', *Symposium presentation at the Biennial Meeting of the Society for Research in Child Development*, Indianapolis, Apr.

Leslie, A. 1987, 'Pretence and representation: the origins of "theory of mind"', *Psychological Review*, vol. 94, pp. 412–26.

Lillard, A. 1993, 'Pretend play skills and the child's theory of mind', *Child Development*, vol. 64, pp. 348–71.

Parten, M. 1932, 'Social participation among preschool children', *Journal of Abnormal Psychology*, vol. 27, pp. 243–69.

Perret-Clermont, A. & Brossard, A. 1985, 'On the interdigitation of social and cognitive processes', in *Social Relationships and Cognitive Development*, Hinde, R., Perret-Clermont, A. & Stevenson-Hinde, J. (eds), Clarendon Press, Oxford.

Piaget, J. 1945, *Play, Dreams and Imitation in Childhood*, Norton, New York.

Piaget, J. 1965, *The Moral Judgement of the Child*, Free Press, New York.

Reifel, S. & Yeatman, J. 1993, 'From category to context: reconsidering classroom play', *Early Childhood Research Quarterly*, vol. 8, pp. 347–67.

Rusher, A., Cross, D. & Ware, A. 1995, 'Infant and toddler play: assessment of exploratory style and development level', *Early Childhood Research Quarterly*, vol. 10, pp. 297–315.

Smilansky, S. 1968, *The Effects of Sociodramatic Play on Disadvantaged Preschool Children*, John Wiley, New York.

Sponseller, D. 1982, 'Play and early education', in *Handbook of Research in Early Childhood Education*, Spodek, B. (ed.), Free Press, New York.

Takhvar, M. & Smith, P. 1990, 'A review and critique of Smilansky's classification scheme and the "nested hierarchy" of play categories', *Journal of Research in Childhood Education*, vol. 4, pp. 112–22.

Part 2

PLAY AND DIVERSITY

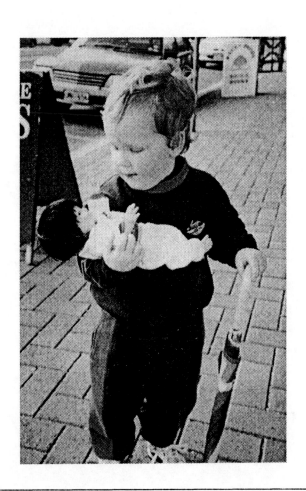

Part 2

Play and Diversity

Part 1 provided us with fundamental information about children's play, development and learning; Part 2, drawing on this, focuses instead on play and diversity. It examines diversity relating to play and children from various cultural backgrounds; Aboriginal children's play; play and gender; and play and ability, including children who are gifted and children with disabilities.

We begin with Lyn Fasoli's story of turtle hunting, in Chapter 4, where the notion of what constitutes play is questioned. This is about two people who initially were 'not a success' when they set up their mobile playgroup at a hostel catering for Aboriginal families. What follows makes engaging reading, and also carries a powerful message for anyone working with young children, and particularly with Aboriginal families and their children. As Elizabeth (Betty) Jones says in the Foreword, 'I wish I had been part of Lyn Fasoli's turtle hunt—the stuff of which dreams are made!' I can't help but agree with her.

This chapter is followed by another that relates to Aboriginal children's play—Chapter 5, written by Veronica Johns. Veronica discusses the differences and similarities between Aboriginal and non-Aboriginal children's play, illustrating her points with observations of various children. Differences between the two groups emerge, for example, in the way Aboriginal children relate to each other and the adults who care for them and in the way they are 'permitted' to take risks. Some of the stories about risk-taking are daunting, and as an adult you cannot help but feel some anxiety, even while acknowledging that taking risks is an important part of growing up in Aboriginal society. I am pleased to include this chapter by Veronica; it seems that little has been written on this topic for early childhood staff, which is regrettable given the number of Aboriginal children now in care outside their extended families.

In Chapter 6, Marilyn Fleer lends support, in part, to Lyn Fasoli and Veronica Johns' messages. Marilyn argues that as a multicultural society we should be learning about play that takes place across cultures, and be sensitive to the cultural meanings acted out through play. Like Sue Dockett in Chapter 3, Marilyn challenges conventional thinking about play, including the belief that Western theories of play can be applied to other cultures. She suggests that if the dominant theories of play are utilised, practitioners may be making misinformed judgments. These issues raised by Marilyn gave rise to debate even before the book went to press (see the Foreword and the Main Editor's note that precedes Marilyn's chapter).

Another thought-provoking chapter follows—Glenda Mac-Naughton's Chapter 7, where she tells us that play is dangerous. She shares some interesting and vivid observations with us as she shows how crossing the gender boundaries in play can be very risky. As children play at 'having babies', 'being monsters' or 'making a hospital' they often show us gender-driven, stereotyped views of female and male roles. Some children, of course, break free of these stereotypes and test out different ways of 'doing gender'—and these are the ones who show us, through the vignettes Glenda includes, just how risky play can be.

Chapter 8 is about play and children who are gifted. Like many other contributors to this book, Kim Tegel and Cathie Harrison point out that play is generally recognised by those involved in the care and education of young children as significant for child development and learning. Most of the contributors in this book indicate their regret that play does not seem to be sufficiently valued in early childhood services, and Kim and Cathie consider it even less valued for the young child who is gifted. They suggest that play is, in fact, crucial for gifted children, and present a persuasive case for open-ended and spontaneous play which best suits their developmental and learning needs. Strategies and resources for supporting rich and valuable play experiences are also outlined.

The section concludes with Chapter 9, written by Barbara (Barb) Creaser. Elizabeth (Betty) Jones says in the Foreword that ever since Barb presented this paper at a Washington State Conference she has been thinking about her observations of children with special needs and how their play is so often interrupted, and the reader will find Barbara's observations both poignant and compelling. Barb suggests that adults should try to adjust more to the children's pace rather than imposing their own, and consider themselves as adding to the children's competence rather than making up for their deficiencies. She argues strongly, as do Cathie Harrison and Kim Tegel, that it is through play that we can promote children's development and learning most effectively—a belief which is at the heart of all the chapters. This is indeed a book that, in Barb's words, is a 'plea for play'.

Chapter 4

Developmentally appropriate play and turtle hunting

Lyn Fasoli

Introduction

Nowadays I would call it a 'multicultural consciousness-raising' experience, but in 1981, when the experience I am about to describe for you occurred, the word 'multicultural' was not part of my vocabulary. When people from different cultures meet, misunderstandings are inevitable, but in this case, they led to learning and increased understanding. Although this experience is somewhat dated, its conditions and characteristics still apply today.

It is important to give some background here. In 1981 I was an early childhood teacher responsible for a mobile playgroup, Fun Bus, catering for socially or geographically isolated families in Darwin in the Northern Territory of Australia. As the only city of significant size within a thousand miles, Darwin attracted many people from outlying regions; and as a city recently devastated by a major cyclone (Cyclone Tracey in 1974), it was home to many young families new to the area. Rapid rebuilding of Darwin over the previous few years had created suburbs which were really just rows of houses or caravan parks perched on treeless dirt landscapes, laced with new asphalt. Shops, churches, community halls, schools and even public telephone booths were being constructed or still on the drawing board. My mission, as I saw it then, was to bring developmentally appropriate activities, information and support to parents and under-school-age children who were isolated, either socially or geographically.

The first locations: the original agenda

These young, isolated, suburban families were the ones my assistant, Mary, and I envisaged as we packed our bus full of playgroup activities, books and pamphlets, resource information and well-meaning advice. By providing them with a non-threatening playgroup, we aimed to help people connect with each other and the rest of Darwin. We had five or six such locations that we visited each week, and for the most part Mary and I pursued our agenda of parent support and education with confidence. We talked to parents about ways children could learn from appropriate early childhood activities and equipment, offered them assistance with problematic behaviour, gave them child development advice, lent them books on special topics, helped them meet each other and form friendships—all typical playgroup experiences. As a service we prided ourselves on our success.

A new location: the script changes

Then we went to a new location, a hostel for Aboriginal families, and found that our formula did not apply. From our first visit we were thrown into confusion and doubt about what we were doing and why. We were definitely not a success!

Many Aboriginal people living in far-flung communities in the top end of Australia came, and still do come, into Darwin for various reasons—shopping, health care, business, visiting relatives, study, sightseeing or to go to the movies. They often stayed at hostels catering for visiting Aboriginal groups, which were organised much like motels. Fun Bus saw an opportunity to work with these families for the same purposes as for others—to provide parent support and education through appropriate early childhood activities. What assumptions we made—and what surprises lay ahead.

The response we received when we set up our playgroup in the courtyard of the hostel on the first day was sobering. Picture the scene: brightly coloured construction toys placed around on a large tarpaulin in the courtyard; paint easels marching along in orderly fashion opposite the bus; a small table with a mound of purple play dough next to the bus; a portable tea urn set up with cups, a packet of biscuits and folding chairs nearby; a library of child care books in the back of the bus; and two small push-bikes waiting to be driven off.

Mary and I sat sipping cups of tea, smiling and inviting people standing in doorways to come and join us. A few small, wide-eyed children gazed at us and could not be enticed to leave their mothers' skirts. Perplexed, mothers gazed at us for a while, smiled and went back to what they had been doing. Occasionally a child wandered out, leapt on a bike and zoomed around the bus. Our hopes were falsely raised when one child played with a toy car for a couple of minutes. It was very awkward; we obviously were not expected or particularly welcome. The management of the hostel had been happy for us to come but the message had not been passed on to the mothers that this service was for them—or perhaps it had. It was hard to tell.

Our second visit was slightly easier. After a vain attempt to strike up a conversation, Mary started painting and handed a paintbrush to one of the mothers. She smiled and started painting a picture on the easel too. Soon most of the other mothers joined in. The children played on the ground close to their feet with whatever was within reach. Although they were friendly, none of the mothers wanted to talk about their children with us. They enjoyed each others' paintings, talked to each other about them and, when we left, taped them on the doors of their rooms.

The third visit was much the same as the previous one, with lots of painting. However, this time an Aboriginal woman told me she was a preschool teacher at one of the communities outside town. After talking for a while, we discovered that we both knew the finger-play 'Where is Thumbkin?' I sang it all the way through, accompanying the words with hand motions. Everyone laughed except the children who watched my hands and mouth, intrigued. Then the preschool teacher sang the same finger-play in her language, Gupapuyngu. I decided to try to learn it. The woman patiently sang it over and over until I succeeded. This created even more hilarity—especially from the children!

Mary and I discussed the progress we had made. We weren't quite sure who was learning what—the playgroup was not a playgroup as we knew it. Communication was still awkward and stilted. In the jargon of the nineties, our learning curves were steep and treacherous as we struggled to make sense of what we were doing. It was perhaps another two or three weeks before we moved into a new phase. The Aboriginal woman who cleaned the hostel came up to us and told us that the women had been talking about us during the past week and had an idea: would we like to go hunting? 'Hunting?' I asked. She suggested that we take the group hunting for long-necked turtles, as if this were the most natural request in the world—which it obviously was to her. Mary and I had a difficult moment as we tried to justify in our own minds how turtle hunting constituted parent support and education. We succeeded. Everyone helped us empty the bus of its usual gear and climbed in with their children. Obviously the playgroup script was changing!

We set off with seven women and more children to Fogg Dam, an hour's drive down the one and only highway out of Darwin. I had no idea what to expect, so I asked them how we would be hunting. 'We'll get long-necked turtle in Fogg Dam,' said one woman. 'How?' I asked. 'We show you,' she responded.

We arrived at the dam, a pristine bird sanctuary covered in large pink–white waterlilies and, according to the signs posted by the Conservation Commission, full of large crocodiles. The women assured me there were no crocodiles on the right-hand side of the dam, only on the left. As I watched them wade into the water I decided they must know what they were doing, so I waded in too. We trudged around up to our armpits in reeds and waterlilies, wriggling our toes in the mud.

Turtle hunting works like this. When you, as wader, feel a stone-like shape underfoot, you swoop down and with a free hand grab what feels like a snake but is actually the neck of the turtle curled back along its shell. Then you pull the turtle up, wring its neck and toss it over the shoulder. It's a very simple procedure. I cannot express my astonishment when I first felt the stone-like shape. I bent down and pulled up a large, wriggling, long-necked turtle. I was ecstatic with accomplishment and surprise. One of the women grabbed it and wrung its neck for me—a relief, as I am not sure my enthusiasm would have carried me through!

We ended up with eight turtles in all. Within ten minutes of landing our catch, the women had made a small yet adequate fire and the turtles were cooking. Although I had proved myself a useful hunter, to my surprise as much as everyone else's, I found my courage evaporating when offered a rare titbit of turtle which the others were eating with relish. I took a grip on myself and ate my portion, watched keenly by the others. I can honestly say it tasted quite good. Lots of laughter and talk followed this, much of it in the women's own language. We sang 'Where is Thumbkin?' in Gupapuyngu on the way back into town.

From this point on Mary and I shelved our preconceived notions of parent support and education, and developmentally appropriate play agenda, and learnt as much as we could from these women and others who visited the hostel. Each week we went hunting for different creatures or vegetation. We hunted goanna, long bums (a kind of shellfish), rock oysters, mangrove worms, mud crabs and so on. I have never learnt so much in such a short time. I learnt the names of things; I learnt to see the potential for food in what had been in my eyes an empty, rather monotonous landscape; I learnt to wait for someone to show me what to do; I learnt to stop asking so many questions. In short, I learnt the way the children were learning—by watching, by being patiently shown, by paying attention and by doing it myself.

Sometimes the women would dance and sing. The children, too, would dance to the rhythms of songs that were so foreign to our ears, and which ended on a beat that sounded very strange but became less so with familiarity. They laughed so hard when Mary and I tried to dance, and shook their heads at our stumbling lack of coordination. It became more natural to talk about children, to share stories about them, and discuss individual differences and developmental milestones.

We never did get back to our original playgroup agenda. 'Developmentally appropriate' activities began to hold a different meaning for me. Children in this playgroup played with mud, not play dough. On the beach, while their mothers caught crabs, children gathered and arranged shells and sticks like natural puzzles. They learnt songs, dances, actions, words and ideas, not because their mothers were playing games with them but because they included them in their adult activities. I began to accept that there might be many ways to learn and many activities that foster development that I had not previously recognised.

I also learnt something important about how people from two different cultures interact. My initial assumptions about what these mothers needed were ethnocentric and narrow. As our relationship developed, I realised that I was only just beginning to understand what they might have wanted from us and our Fun Bus. I cannot know precisely what these women learnt from us, but I am sure that they acquired information about children's services available, and certainly some idea of our views on child-rearing, as well as getting to know Mary and myself as people. I realised that, far from being isolated, these women were connected with this part of the world and each other in a way I could not have imagined prior to this experience. In fact, Mary and I were the ones who were isolated; we were the ones who gained the support and education for living more effectively in this rich landscape and varied culture.

Conclusion

The transition from our original agenda to a more flexible one may sound smooth now, but at the time it wasn't easy to abandon our prescribed roles as playgroup leaders. We kept trying to rationalise what we were doing with what we thought we were supposed to be doing. It took us a long time to realise that what we were doing was entirely legitimate—that is, learning with humility the importance of not holding preconceived notions about education. We were learning to offer a service in a culturally relevant way. At the time we did not broadcast our 'hunting' activities within our organisation, as we were fairly certain of receiving criticism. In hindsight, I think that we should have explained them openly and honestly, and passed on the lessons that we learnt from our experience long ago.

For further thought and discussion

1. Have you ever had an experience, like the one described in this chapter, where you were confused or felt uneasy about what you were doing with young children in your program? Discuss this with a friend or colleague, and try to identify what you did—or could have done—to create a better match between your program and the children in it.

2. What do you know about the children using your program? Look at the list that follows and identify any gaps in your knowledge of them:

   - country of origin;
   - language/s spoken;
   - parents' competence in oral and written English;
   - eating and sleeping patterns/arrangements, and expectations at home;
   - important holidays, celebrations and cultural responsibilities;
   - attitude of the family towards play;
   - playmates of the child at home;
   - usual play activities and materials used at home;
   - the family's attitude towards discipline;
   - responsibilities of the child at home;
   - expectations held for the child.

   (List adapted from Arthur, Beecher, Dockett, Farmer & Richards, 1993, pp. 40–52)

3. Choose one child in your program who comes from a culture different from your own. Using the list above, write down what you already know about him or her. Now use the list as a guide to talk to this child's parent or family member.

4. With this information, how might you change your program to better cater for this child's play interests and abilities?
5. Consider the outdoor environment near your service. How much do you know about the plants and animals that live there? How could you find out more about them? Do you know anyone who could teach you how Aboriginal people have used or use the plants and animals in your region? How could you use natural materials in your service to expand play opportunities for children?

Reference

Arthur, L., Beecher, B., Dockett, S., Farmer, S. & Richards, E. 1993, *Programming and Planning in Early Childhood Settings*, Harcourt Brace Jovanovich, Sydney.

Chapter 5

Embarking on a journey: Aboriginal children and play

Veronica Johns

Introduction

> While playing, children are expressing themselves and who they are each through their skills, their thoughts and their behaviours. (Van Diermen & Johns 1995, p. 15)

Through play, Aboriginal children embark on a journey of learning and growing that takes them through time and space as they take on various roles, including people, animals and symbols.

A three-year-old walks around the play yard with a doll held to her *nga nga* (breast).

A carer and her group of three toddlers crawl around the floor on all fours mimicking dogs.

Planning for play

As carers, it is important that we are able to understand the needs of young Aboriginal children at play. We are told that it takes a lot of observation on our part to get to know the children in our care, and that we can learn as much from watching and listening as from talking and asking questions. We are also taught that time and attention are necessary to set the scene for children's play. I agree that we need to observe children and can often set the scene for their play, but would argue that lots of play experiences can be simple and valuable and do not always require us, the adults, to set the scene.

> A group of four children aged between 18 months and two years are out in the yard with a carer. As I walk outside I hear excited squeals and, looking towards the sound, I see two children hiding behind hanging palm fronds.
>
> A four-year-old boy has detached himself from the rest of the group and is swinging quietly on the swing, alone. My guess is that this child needed some space to play by himself and was able to find that space.

Play can be both spontaneous and planned, but most importantly it is about being free—free to choose one's own direction, free to take a risk and have a go. It is about belonging, wanting to achieve and putting thoughts into action. It is about the enjoyment of splashing in a puddle of water with other children; the sense of achievement you get when you can jump from a high spot like the bigger kids; and the peace of being held by a carer and absently rubbing at her *nga nga* as you watch the other children playing around you.

Characteristics of Aboriginal children's play

Although all children's play is similar, regardless of whether they are Aboriginal or non-Aboriginal, areas of difference may include: being granted the 'permission' to take risks; play being seen as a survival mechanism; the acceptance of humour; play fighting; and the responsibilities of children to each other and to adults. Let us look at each area in turn.

Risk-taking

In a setting with mixed-age groups, the younger children can be challenged by the older children's play.

> William, 21 months, repeatedly climbs onto stepping logs and jumps off. He has obviously watched the older children do this and is now imitating them. My heart is in my mouth as I see him crawling onto logs that range from 21–54 centimetres in height. In my mind I see him going head-first over the other side. I move forward quickly, asking him to hang on and I'll help him. Too late—he has manoeuvred himself up and around, and jumped onto the gym mat in a matter of seconds!

This is just one example of a child taking a risk. In Aboriginal society, risk-taking is considered an important learning process for children, and is quite acceptable as long as an adult is present and the children know the rules.

As carers, we shouldn't try to stop children from doing something they are used to doing at home and about which their families are not worried. Children rarely get hurt although toddlers, of course, may fall as they try to run at a great pace. This is considered a normal part of development: they have to fall over in order to become more competent.

I was out in a remote community recently and observed a two-year-old trying to prise the side bags from a toy motorbike. To make his task easier, he had taken a meat knife from the kitchen. His grand-father was sitting nearby and occasionally glanced up at the child. The child continued with what he was doing and, judging by certain expressions, at times missed the bike and hit his finger. I gather the knife was not too sharp as he didn't cut himself.

The grandfather was, I would say, respecting his grandchild by allowing him to do something for himself and learn first-hand about the tool he had chosen to work with—a challenging experience that he would have had a tough time learning.

This is not an experience that we would allow in a child care centre, but there are other ones that we can assist children with.

Out in the bush one day a toddler stood at the bottom of a tree. He was looking up into the branches and crying. He seemed to want to be up the tree with the older children. He wasn't consoled until I propped him up astride a low limb.

On other occasions we may have to stand back to let children experiment on their own.

A small group of three-year-olds are climbing up a frame. They stand on the top, balance and jump into the sandpit. A two-year-old is watching, then all of a sudden is crawling up the frame. I reach out to help him. He pushes my hand away and, although the words are unintelli-

> gible to me, I know from his tone and action that he doesn't want my help.
>
> I stand behind, close at hand. I feel anxious, but confidence and determination emanate from this child as he climbs the frame, jumps into the sandpit, then repeats the action over and over again.

It was important that I allowed this child the experience of getting better at climbing and positioning himself to jump. This continued for about ten minutes, with the older children joining in. As adults, we are often faced with this type of situation as children become 'ready' to tackle new challenges.

> Another child watched, apparently wanting to join in this play but looking apprehensive. I offered my hand to help him and within a short time he was jumping too.

While the children were jumping from quite a height, I watched. When more children starting joining in the game, I had to make some rules—so it became the Olympic Games. The children took turns, while I called out, 'Okay, let's have the next contestant!'

Games like this one shouldn't be stopped, but at times there need to be rules, and the children need to know the reasons for them. If any rules are made, they shouldn't be restrictive and the atmosphere should remain relaxed.

Survival mechanism

> From a very early age children are told about their country and what it means to them. They learn to use their senses to 'read' their country and listen to what it says to them. (Van Diermen & Johns 1995, p. 18)

Play can be a survival mechanism. Children's observation skills are developing all the time as they tune into the environment. They are acquiring an awareness of where they are heading and what they need to do, which is critical both as a link with the land and for survival. To survive you have to be aware. Although many Aboriginal children and their families may not be living on their land, or may have lost it, it means a great deal to them and they are still in tune with it.

Play as a survival mechanism also means responsibility. Children have to be responsible for themselves, and they achieve this through playing and exploring their environment. Through their play they learn about:

- directions—knowing where to go and how to get there;
- observations—assessing the situation at hand and looking for what or who is familiar;
- decisions—calculating what to do;
- actions—following through with an action or task.

Humour

There are times when the children enjoy 'getting the best' of the adult.

A four-year-old 'escapes' into my office during a transition between lunch and waiting to go home. He distracts an adult who is asking him where he is supposed to be, by pointing to the computer that has words passing from right to left across the screen. As each word passes, the adult reads 'smiling' (pause) 'happy' (pause) 'people' (pause) 'work' (pause) 'here'.

Although this was not a play environment, this is an example of a child at play. He had 'snuck' away, found a distraction for the adult and played with words. What fun! We don't always have to be the ones in charge. Children love getting the better of adults and in Aboriginal culture this is not seen as disrespectful.

Play fighting

Play fighting, which can be very physical, often worries staff who are non-Aboriginal or who haven't had much experience with young Aboriginal children. Children will play at fighting, but there is still respect and caring. It rarely turns nasty and then only if the child isn't family. The respect and caring shown by children has to do with survival, and they feel that no matter what else they must show respect. They know that there are rules to be followed and that, if they go too far, they will be frowned upon.

Responsibility

There is an outside-school-hours care program next door to the long day care program. All the children feel that they belong in both places. The older children watch after and care for the younger children. They don't need to be asked; it is a practice that they grew up with and is role modelled for them by others.

Older children feel good about caring for the younger ones and taking responsibility for them. Often the babies become the 'dolls' for the older children and I see, for example, the older girls feeding them, carrying them around, disciplining them or putting them to bed. This practice becomes important in later life because, while the children are the responsibility of the whole community, it is the women's role to be directly responsible for them. These children are, therefore, learning vital skills and responsibilities through play.

I recall a day during National Aboriginal and Torres Strait Islanders Week. Lots of activities were set up in the park by the beach. Observing them, I realised that groups of children from non-Aboriginal child care services were moving together as a single unit, accompanied by an adult. The children from the Aboriginal child care service, however, moved around as they wished, unaccompanied by the adults who were watching out for all children as their responsibility, including those from other groups.

The child mentioned earlier, being held by a carer and absently rubbing at her *nga nga* while watching other children playing, is an expression of a relationship that is special, and not one you would usually see in a non-Aboriginal service. While the carer is not this child's biological mother, her bond with the child is as close as if she were.

Understanding families and relationships is critical when working with young Aboriginal children. O'Donoghue broadly defines the family as 'the various arrangements people make to ensure that the young are nurtured and people are looked after', and points out that 'the extended family is very important in Aboriginal society' (O'Donoghue, cited in Creaser & Dau 1995, p. 124). The family helps the child acquire, through play, knowledge that is particularly important in Aboriginal society; that is, to know:

- who they are;
- where they fit in;
- what is expected of them (Van Diermen & Johns 1995, p. 14).

Conclusion

As adults, we need to plan for children's play, and set the scene for their play after observing them, yet be sensitive to the fact that play is often initiated by children. Such play, whether planned by the children themselves or spontaneous, is as valuable as that planned by staff.

For Aboriginal children, as for all children, play forms a basis for learning. Their actions and achievements in play enable them to extend themselves and take risks, as well as finding out about themselves and the environment around them.

For further thought and discussion

1. Think about the relationship between play and time. Is play a survival mechanism that links past, present and future? How does play in the past relate to play in the present? Does play in the present and the past give meaning to the future?
2. Observe children at play in the service where you work or are undertaking your field experience. Are there instances of spontaneous play, initiated by children? After you have observed the play episode, think about the value of the play.
3. Re-read the section in this chapter on Aboriginal children and humour. If you are not working—nor have experienced working—with Aboriginal children, how do you think you would have reacted to this situation?
4. This chapter suggests that, most importantly, play is 'about being free—free to choose one's own direction, free to take a risk and have a go'. Do you allow children to take risks within a framework of safety? Do the safety rules in this framework actually support risk-taking behaviour?

References

O'Donoghue, L., cited in Dau, E. 'Exploring families: the diversity and the issues', in Creaser, B. & Dau, E. 1995, *The Anti-Bias Approach in Early Childhood*, HarperEducational, Sydney.

Van Diermen, S. & Johns, V. 1995, *From the Flat Earth: A Guide for Child Care Staff Caring for Aboriginal Children*, Children's Services Resource and Advisory Program (Northern Region), Darwin.

Chapter 6

Universal fantasy: the domination of Western theories of play

Marilyn Fleer

Main Editor's note

The content of this chapter is, I believe thought-provoking and worthy of inclusion in this book. It does, however, challenge some of the assumptions made in other chapters, where the importance of Western-style socio-dramatic play in childhood is usually taken for granted. If this is your view, you may choose to pass over this chapter to the later ones. However, I hope that it will lead many readers to consider and debate the issues raised. As Fleer herself says, 'this chapter is designed to stimulate thinking and raise issues, and does not seek to present a conclusive and definitive argument'.

However, I would like to point out that, in advocating play, it is important to remember that the activities of children vary greatly, not only between individuals but also between cultures. Play is learnt behaviour, acquired as children interact with older members of the society in which they live.

Fleer asks us to look at our emphasis on representational play as ethnocentric, and ask, 'is it relevant for all children living in Australia?' In a multicultural society, however, children face two tasks: to become competent members of their home culture, and to move competently into the dominant culture reflected in, for example, schools—where representation of experience is what the curriculum is all about.

Not all programs set the same priorities but, for many children, early childhood programs provide a bridge in which the mastery of representational play can play a significant part in developing bicultural competence. It is, I believe, a sign of a healthy early childhood profession that we debate these issues. May the debate continue!

Introduction

During the twentieth century, the play activities of children have been studied, labelled and categorised as the basis of theory development. Piaget, Smilansky and Parten, among others, theorised about children at play. Their theories, which are mostly developmental in nature, tell us a great deal about the play activities of children from Western countries—but are they relevant for all children living in Australia? Can they, for example, help us understand the play of children from Asian communities? Are they relevant to Aboriginal children living in traditionally orientated communities? Should we even consider fitting the activities of Aboriginal children into such frameworks in the first instance? Similarly, what do we understand about specific cultural groups' interactive patterns with their children and their implications for play—as defined in a Western sense?

This chapter seeks to explore these issues with a view to first, relabelling much of what we consider to be 'play' as 'Western play'; second, examining cross-cultural research for evidence of a range of interactive patterns relevant to play; and finally to rethinking and broadening the term 'play' from being a specific Western pedagogical tool to one that is culturally inclusive. This chapter is designed to stimulate thinking and raise issues, and does not seek to present a conclusive and definitive argument.

The play activities of children

The play activities of children have been strongly supported in Western societies. Their educational and social benefits have been extensively documented and need not be elaborated upon here. This chapter considers the broad spectrum of play activities of children. However, an important discriminator in the discussions that follow relates to the presence, and therefore nature, of 'representational play'. As Feitelson says: 'Representational play is characterised by the fact that a certain imaginative play theme is the mainspring of activity. The nature of the theme can change in time as the play activity continues, but some kind of content is always indicated by any means whatsoever.' (Feitelson 1977, p. 6)

According to Feitelson, this type of play activity is also referred to as 'make-believe' or 'imaginative' play (Singer 1973), 'socio-dramatic' play (Smilansky 1968) and 'thematic' play (Feitelson & Ross 1973). It has also been termed 'symbolic play' (Gaskins & Göncü 1988), 'free-flow play', 'free play', 'pretend play' or 'ludic play' (Bruce 1991).

Smilansky and Shefatya (1990, cited in Dockett 1995, p. 2) detail elements of 'socio-dramatic play' as imitative role play, make-believe with objects, make-believe with actions and situations, persistence, interaction, and verbal communication. Finer discriminations of play activity allow researchers and practitioners to discuss the complexity of play events. This chapter highlights differences across cultures by giving due consideration to describing play activities within each culture.

Paradigm shifts in the conceptualisation of play

As most early childhood specialists would be aware, prior to Rousseau's work, play was not given serious consideration. Indeed, many theorists and philosophers either ignored this area entirely in the development of individuals or considered it merely practice work and, as such, not significant. Since the 1870s, three main values have been identified in the study of play:

- its cognitive value;
- its emotional value;
- its social value.

According to Cohen (1987), many theorists such as Froebel and Montessori did not see play as a valuable activity in its own right, but simply as a means through which children could be taught more formal skills. With increased attention being given to play, many psychologists began to examine animal behaviour, drawing analogies with human play behaviour (Bruner, Jolly & Sylva 1976).

In his book *Play, Dreams and Imitation in Childhood* (1962), Piaget reports on how his children 'played' at home and with their parents. However, most research does not concentrate on the naturalistic context, but rather seeks to isolate and identify stages of development in play within contrived laboratory contexts or naturalistic contexts adapted through introduced toys and instruments (Cohen 1987; Nicolopoulou 1993; Sutton-Smith 1980). These methodological issues, as related to past and present research activity into play, are currently under scrutiny (Nicolopoulou 1993).

More recent research by MacNaughton (1995), which utilises naturalistic settings (preschools) to examine play, shows how gender-driven patterns of interaction determine the type and direction of children's play. This suggests that children's play could be more strongly influenced by gender-driven patterns of behaviour which are culturally determined than by innate characteristics—as has been argued when animal behaviour is examined. The implications for educators are clear—play can be viewed as socially constructed and hence learnt.

The learning of play

Maclane is eight years old and lives in a remote and traditionally orientated Aboriginal community. Maclane attends a one-room school with one teacher (with a Western background) and one Aboriginal Education Worker. During the morning he moves over to the 'dramatic play' area and puts on a tie. He drapes a shawl over his shoulders. He then takes a frilly white hat and puts it on his head. He selects a yellow handbag and holds it gently between his hands. He then promenades around the classroom. Children spontaneously laugh, point and shout. He continues walking around the room, smiling broadly and enjoying the responses. After 15 minutes he settles at a table and begins to interact with the materials and children. He remains dressed in the mix of male and female clothing for the entire school day.

The 3–12-year-old children in the schoolroom regularly use the dress-up materials for promenading. The stove and bedding (replicas of items in the children's environment) in the room and diverse range of dress-up clothes are not used for role playing Mums and Dads or Aunty and Uncle—as often happens in Western communities. Similarly, the need to dress as male or female is not evident in how the children dress up (Humffray 1997). This highlights how the Western view of the arrangement and use of a dramatic play area is not necessarily utilised by Aboriginal children as expected. In this cross-cultural context, Maclane and the other children bring to the setting their views of how to play with the materials provided. Vygotsky argues that a belief in 'free play' is nonsense:

> Where there is an imaginary situation in play, there are rules—
> not rules that are formulated in advance and change during the

course of the game but ones that stem from an imaginary situation. Therefore, the notion that a child *can behave in an imaginary situation without rules is simply inaccurate.* (Vygotsky 1978, p. 95; my italics)

According to Vygotsky, there is nothing 'free' about 'play'. The play themes originate from the child's culture, and the interactions between children are based on a shared or common knowledge (Edwards & Mercer 1987) about the context, storyline and appropriate interactive patterns. For example, in Feitelson (1977) meta-analysis of cross-cultural studies of representational play and a significant amount of ethnographic research supports the learnt nature of play. Learnt play in these contexts relates to the active encouragement (and sometimes demonstration) by adults of appropriate play activities for children:

> . . . work in the Soviet Union (El'konin 1966; Chauncey 1969), Israel (Smilansky 1968; Feitelson 1972) and the United States (Feitelson & Ross 1973; Freyberg 1973) stressed *the learned aspect of representational play.* Citing work by Fradkina, El'konin (1966) maintained that symbolic play activity does not develop spontaneously. It arises, instead, in interaction with adults who suggest it. (Feitelson 1977, p. 13; my italics)

Research with American, Mexican, and Indonesian toddlers demonstrated that:

> . . . mothers who valued play for its educational and cognitive benefits were more likely to join their children's play activity and to provide props and suggestions that encouraged the expression of pretend play than mothers who viewed children's play as amusement or imitation of adult models . . . (Farver, Kim, & Lee 1995, p. 1089)

In research conducted by Farver, Kim & Lee, it is found that 'Anglo-American children, whose mothers believed that play is important for children's learning and development, engaged in more pretend play in the home than Korean–American children, whose mothers considered play to be a way to escape boredom or to amuse children' (Farver, Kim & Lee 1995, p. 1097).

Similarly, differences in mother–infant interactions are noted by Hamilton. He finds that only 8.5 per cent of Aboriginal Anbarra infants interact with objects (other than food):

> Where the European mother uses objects in the environment as a means of distracting, pacifying and amusing the child, offering both toys and everyday items in the house to be accepted and explored by the child, the Aboriginal mother seldom does this. The child's emotional contentment is assured by social interaction with people, notably the mother, mediated by some form of oral experience; there is little room for objects to become of more than momentary significance. (Hamilton 1981, pp. 98–9)

Although Hamilton does not seek to determine how mothers and infants played, the observations illustrate significant differences between Western and Aboriginal cultures. Support for the learnt nature of play themes and interactions is gaining wider acceptance as further research is conducted (eg MacNaughton 1996). If play is learnt, whether through adults or peers, then the predetermined developmental path in play as advocated by Parten (1932) or Piaget (1962), for example, needs to be questioned. Are these developmental theories of play helpful in analysing the activities of children today? Could we reconsider their play activities in different ways? Given the changing context, how useful are the theories of play in guiding educators working together to support children's learning in play-based programs?

In the literature on play this century, two waves of research are evident (Nicolopoulou 1993). The first wave of research is centred on the individualistic nature of play. Generated by Piaget's work, this research examines the socio-cultural factors associated with play, although Nicolopoulou (1993) argues that it has not been adequately considered in current theories of play. The second wave of research, based on the work of Vygotsky, to whose thesis the socio-cultural dimension of play is central, has been utilised in recent years to guide researchers. According to Nicolopoulou, 'this second stream of research has thus far taken up the Vygotskian "inspiration" in a limited and inadequate way' (Nicolopoulou 1993, p. 1). This research focuses predominantly on interaction, and does not take into account the wider socio-cultural elements that define and shape the 'play' context (Nicolopoulou 1993). The play activities of children in relation to their cultural practices need to be understood better, and the cultural meanings enacted through play examined.

Characteristics of Western and non-Western play activities

In multicultural communities, such as those in Australia and New Zealand, it cannot be automatically assumed Western theories of play are relevant for all children. Consider, for instance, this description of Australian Aboriginal children from traditionally orientated rural communities at play: 'the intense fantasy games which European boys of this age indulge in, playing 'explorers' or 'pirates' or 'doctors', with elaborately arranged role structures and a predetermined set of behavioural sequences, were apparently absent' (in the Anbarra Aboriginal community) (Hamilton 1981, p. 132).

Clearly, social pretend play is not a feature of Anbarra children's play, where boys' play is centred around exploring the environment and their developing physical skills. Girls also participate in these activities, although not to the same extent. Hamilton notes:

> Small groups of young girls, usually no more than four in number, frequently go off alone into the bush or to the beach, and usually return with a small amount of food to share with their female relations, having eaten what they wanted themselves wherever they gathered the food. When walking outside the Settlement area, I frequently saw little parties of girls who had caught a lizard or bird and were cooking by their own fire . . . Girls tend to be more in evidence around the camp area than boys of the same age, and when they do go off alone they do not go as far afield. (Hamilton 1981, p. 104)

Much of the literature on play used in education today is derived from research conducted from a Western perspective and collected in Western contexts. Where cross-cultural data is combined with data from Western communities, it reveals that many children from lower socio-economic groups do not engage in 'representational play'. Interestingly, many of these studies include in their sample of a lower socio-economic group, children from non-Western cultures, and in their higher socio-economic group, children from Western cultures (Smith 1977). For example, Smilansky (1968) studies disadvantaged preschool children mostly from the Middle East and North Africa and compares them with children from high socio-cultural backgrounds from European countries. She notes that, 'we were, however, astonished to learn that children from the low socio-cultural strata play very little and most of them do not participate in socio-dramatic play at all' (Smilansky 1968, p. 4).

Smilansky's findings can be attributed in part to cultural differences rather than simply socio-economic factors. The assumption inherent in Smilansky's interpretation of her results is that of a deficit rather than a difference model (Cole & Bruner 1971). It cannot be assumed that a Western research design, and the findings of such research, can be applied in cross-cultural contexts (Ariel & Sever 1980). Smilansky's interpretation highlights how easily Western researchers and practitioners who value representational or socio-dramatic play can measure the absence or presence of this type of activity in non-Western children without considering the overall cultural context in which it exists.

Ethnographic and anthropological studies of family and community groups in cross-cultural settings provide some useful and interesting data on the play activities of children. According to Feitelson (1977), archaeological findings from prehistoric sites and ethnographic studies conducted over the previous 50 years provide evidence that representational play does occur in non-Western communities. However, Feitelson (1977) also argues that the evidence is severely flawed. For example, archaeologists presume that toy-like artefacts, such as miniature clay figures of humans and implements, were intended for children's use. In her extensive meta-analysis of cross-cultural literature, Feitelson (1977) shows that there is significant evidence to suggest that many of these artefacts were primarily intended for use in rituals.

Ethnographic studies provide evidence that types of play activities in Western cultures differ from those in non-Western cultures. Rather than utilising their free time for representational play, Feitelson argues that 'in terms of representational play, children in ascriptive game cultures imitate the behaviour of their elders: *they replicate but do not transform*' (Feitelson 1977, p. 8; my italics). In their descriptions of representational play activities in small, relatively homogeneous agricultural communities in Africa and India, observers stress time and again the close link between adult activities and their imitation in children's play (Feitelson 1977, p. 8).

Feitelson (1977) cites research by Mead (1946) from the Solomon Islands, New Guinea, Argentina and Bali; by Nessa (1970) from East

Pakistan; by Wiener (1969) from Katanga; by Nzioki (1967) from Kamba, East Africa; and by Fortes (1938) from Taleland. Overall Feitelson (1977) indicates that the research suggests that the play activities described are short-lived and, when compared with those of their Western peers, show a discontinuity and lack of complexity (Feitelson 1977, p. 8).

Mead's (1930) extensive ethnographic work indicates that 'despite ample free time and abundant natural materials ready at hand, Manus children did not engage in imaginative play . . . The play of young children she observed reminded her of that "of young puppies or kittens"' (Feitelson 1977, p. 9). Feitelson found that in Middle-Eastern communities, 'mothers not only did not model play or provide play objects but felt called upon to *interfere actively when imaginative elements cropped up in a play situation*' (Feitelson 1977, p. 13; my italics). Similarly, Ariel and Sever show in their research that 'important aspects of the content, structure and development of individual and social play are not universal, but culture-bound' (Ariel & Sever 1980, p. 174).

Later ethnographic research by Gaskins and Göncü provides further evidence that the nature of play varies from one culture to another:

> . . . play represents something fundamentally different for the Mayan child than it does for the American child. First, Mayan play themes are exclusively about adult activities that are frequently observed . . . Secondly, there is little elaboration or introduction of variation or complexity during the course of play. Scripts and roles are repeated over and over almost ritualised . . . Mayan children do not pretend to be something other than people . . . They do not create imaginary people or things in their play . . . They rely on actual objects or co-players to fill symbolic roles. (Gaskins & Göncü 1992, p. 32)

The research of Gaskins and Göncü also suggests that Mayan adults do not 'participate in or seem to be entertained by children's symbolic play. They do not encourage their children to pretend, do not offer props or suggestions for their play, nor reward them for it with praise or attention' (Gaskins & Göncü 1992, p. 32). Unfortunately, their research does not specify the context in which their observations of children and adults took place. Gaskins and Göncü go on to say that in Mayan culture play is 'not valued by adults in its own right', and that 'men usually prefer to see their children engaged in some productive activity. Women typically tend to permit their children to play some, but they value play only for the work time it provides them, not for any particular value that play might have for the children' (Gaskins & Göncü 1992, p. 32).

These studies highlight not just the learnt nature of representational play and its active encouragement or discouragement by family members, but the differing play activities of children across various cultures:

> The studies reviewed so far establish that not only were there great differences in the quality of representational play among children growing up in different societies but that in some societies this mode of play was almost non-existent. The style of play in any one society was by no means a random occurrence but was closely linked to its social make-up and the role of young children in it. (Feitelson 1977, p. 9)

The implications for educators

The implications of this research for all educators, especially those of Western background, are enormous. There are three areas in particular that need consideration: defining the term 'play', examining its nature, and analysing one's own beliefs.

Defining 'play'

Educators need to move beyond their own cultural preconceptions about play and reconsider what it really is. They need to ask themselves:

1. Is social pretend or fantasy play important?
2. Why is it that social pretend play is valued differently across various cultures?
3. Are there cognitive preferences in play or are preferences socially and culturally determined?

Examining the nature of play

Educators need to look closely at what their children are doing and investigate whether or not they all play and, if so, how. They need to ask themselves:

1. What play experiences have children had prior to attending preschool, child care or school?
2. What value do the children's families place on play?
3. Over time, how do particular children mostly play?
4. Is there a range of ways of playing in a group?

Analysing one's own beliefs

Educators need to reflect upon their own belief system. If children do not engage in social pretend or fantasy play, how do they feel about it? Educators need to think through the following questions:

1. Should they tutor children to engage in social pretend or fantasy play?
2. How can they further develop individual children's existing expertise and cultural experience in play?
3. How can children contribute to each other's play?

In general terms, educators need to move beyond Western theories of play when analysing what they observe. It is important to note the range of expressions of pretend play evident across cultures. In this process, the observations made of children over time need to be considered in light of the value placed upon play. Similarly, planning for children's play should involve educators recognising and supporting different cultures or taking a multicultural approach. In the observing, analysing and planning processes, educators should keep in mind the children's culture.

Conclusion

Should educators, therefore, support ethnocentric play or inclusive play? It would seem that representational play, like all other social behaviour, is situated in the cultural traditions of a particular society. The play activities of children—regardless of their type—are culturally defined, valued and interpreted, and exist, in large part, as a result of cultural practices.

Ariel and Sever argue that the 'content, structure and development of individual and social play are not universal, but culture-bound', and that this 'severely restricts the scope of theories in the structure and development of play, such as Piaget's (1972, Part 2) or Erikson's (eg 1940)' (Ariel & Sever 1980, p. 174). If we accept this, it follows that the developmental pathway or framework used to describe play should be culturally specific, and that theories of play as defined by Parten, Smilansky, Piaget and others should be considered within the cultural context in which they were conceptualised. Applying Western theories of play across cultures is, therefore, deemed inappropriate, since they could construct a deficit model for non-Western children when compared with Western children, and provide silences instead of illuminating culturally specific play activities of children.

There is a need for ethnographic research to be conducted on contemporary Australian children from a range of cultural backgrounds—focusing on interactions within a range of socio-cultural contexts. As a multicultural community, we have a great deal to learn about the range of culturally specific play activities of children who come into our care. We need to understand and value the differing types of play that take place across cultures, as well as the cultural meanings enacted through play. If we do not, we risk utilising a deficit model for our observations of non-Western children; that is, judging children's play, either consciously or unconsciously, by culturally inappropriate standards.

For further thought and discussion

1. What culturally specific play have you noticed when observing children in your centre or elsewhere?
2. How useful do you find contemporary theories of play for interpreting the play activities of children from multicultural Australia?
3. How do the various theories of play help us understand the cultural meanings enacted through play?
4. Do you consider gender issues within the cultural construction of play for our own and other cultures?
5. What is the role of the adult in culturally specific play?

References

Ariel, S. & Sever, I. 1980, 'Play in the desert and play in the town: on play activities of Bedouin Arab children', in Schwartzman, H. B. (ed.), *Play and Culture*, Leisure Press, New York.
Bruce, T. 1991, *Time to Play in Early Childhood Education*, Hodder & Stoughton, London.

Bruner, J., Jolly, H. & Sylva, K. 1976, *Play*, Penguin, Harmondsworth.

Cohen, D. 1987, *The Development of Play*, Croom Helm, Sydney.

Cole, M. & Bruner, J. 1971, 'Cultural differences and inferences about psychological processes', *American Psychologists*, vol. 26, pp. 867–94.

Dockett, S. 1995, *You Make Me Alive! Developing Understanding through Play*, Australian Early Childhood Resource Booklet, Australian Early Childhood Association, Canberra.

Edwards, D. & Mercer, N. 1987, *Common Knowledge*, Methuen, New York.

Farver, J. A. M., Kim, Y. K. & Lee, Y. 1995, 'Cultural differences in Korean and Anglo–American preschoolers' social interaction and play behaviours', *Child Development*, vol. 66, pp. 1089–97.

Feitelson, D. 1977, 'Cross-cultural studies of representational play', in Tizard, B. & Harvey, D. (eds), *Biology of Play*, William Heinemann Medical Books Ltd, London.

Gaskins, S. & Göncü, A. 1988, 'Children's play as representation and imagination: the case of Piaget and Vygotsky', *The Quarterly Newsletter of the Laboratory of Comparative Human Cognition*, vol. 10, no. 4, pp. 104–7.

Gaskins, S. & Göncü, A. 1992, 'Cultural variation in play: a challenge to Piaget and Vygotsky', *The Quarterly Newsletter of the Laboratory of Comparative Human Cognition*, vol. 14, no. 2, pp. 31–5.

Hamilton, A. 1981, *Nature and Nurture: Aboriginal Child Rearing in North-Central Arnhem Land*, Australian Institute of Aboriginal Studies, Canberra.

Humffray, J. 1997, preschool teacher, ACT Department of Education (personal communications).

MacNaughton, G. 1996, 'A poststructuralist analysis of learning in early childhood settings', in Fleer, M. (ed.), *DAPcentrism: Challenging Developmentally Appropriate Practice*, Australian Early Childhood Association, Canberra.

Mead, M. 1930, *Growing up in New Guinea*, William Morrow, New York.

Nicolopoulou, A. 1993, 'Play, cognitive development and the social world: Piaget, Vygotsky, and beyond', *Human Development*, vol. 36, pp. 1–23.

Parten, M. 1932, 'Social participation among pre-school children', *Journal of Abnormal and Social Psychology*, vol. 27, pp. 243–69.

Piaget, J. 1962, *Play, Dreams and Imitation in Childhood*, Norton, New York.

Smilansky, S. 1968, *The Effects of Sociodramatic Play on Disadvantaged Preschool Children*, John Wiley, New York.

Smith, P. 1977, 'Social and fantasy play in young children', in Tizard B. & Harvey, D. (eds), *Biology of Play*, William Heinemann Medical Books Ltd, London.

Sutton-Smith, B. 1980, 'A supportive theory of play', in Schwartzmann, H. (ed.), *Play and Culture*, Leisure Press, New York.

Vygotsky, L. 1978, 'The role of play in development', in Cole, M., Steiner, J., Scribner, S. & Souberman, J. (eds/trans.), *Mind in Society, The Development of Higher Psychological Processes*, Harvard University Press, London.

Acknowledgment

Funding from the Jean Denton Memorial and Lillian de Lissa Scholarship for this chapter enabled this research into cross-cultural play activities of children to take place.

This chapter is based on a paper printed in the *Australian Journal of Early Childhood*, and is included here with permission from the Australian Early Childhood Association. The original version can be found in the *Australian Journal of Early Childhood*, vol. 21, no. 2, pp. 12–17), under the title of 'Theories of play: are they ethnocentric or inclusive?'

Chapter 7

Even pink tents have glass ceilings: crossing the gender boundaries in pretend play

Glenda MacNaughton

Introduction

Children's pretend play is rich with information about how they understand gender relations. As they play at 'having babies', 'being monsters' or 'making a hospital', children show others what they think girls and women can and should do, and what they think boys and men can and should do. Often young children demonstrate narrow and gender-stereotyped views of such roles, although others break free from them and test out different ways of 'doing gender' in their pretend play. These children test out possibilities of crossing traditional gender boundaries and of how it feels to be seen by others as being different to the norm. For instance, some girls imagine 'piloting space-ships' rather than 'being mums' and some boys imagine 'being mums' rather than 'being monsters'.

Crossing traditional gender boundaries in this way can be very risky in pretend play. Several vignettes of children's pretend play used here show that risks include peer rejection, peer aggression and loneliness. This chapter aims to help staff recognise when children are most likely to encounter these risks in their pretend play, and offer them a six-point plan for minimising these risks. An active risk-minimisation plan can support children who choose to cross the gender boundaries and support staff wishing to promote gender equity in their program. A successful risk-minimisation plan rests on staff understanding the role of power in pretend play. To help staff address this, I begin by drawing on the work of Michel Foucault.

Pretend play and power

> Power is everywhere.
> Everything is dangerous.

So believed the French social theorist Michel Foucault who died of AIDS in 1985, hailed by many academics and political activists as one of the most influential and controversial social theorists of the twentieth century. His biographer wrote:

> In a variety of academic fields, scholars were grappling with the implications of his empirical research and pondering the abstract questions that he raised: about the reach of power and the limits of knowledge, about the origins of moral responsibility, the foundations of modern government, and the nature of personal identity. (Miller 1993, p. 13)

His work has also revolutionised how many early childhood academics understand children's learning and play (Walkerdine 1981; Davies 1989; Alloway 1995; MacNaughton 1995(a); Grieshaber 1996; Danby 1996). These academics have drawn on, refined and adapted Foucault's theories of knowledge construction and power to argue that power is everywhere in children's play and much of what children play is indeed dangerous.

Power consists of, in the first instance, the ability to make things happen—and we generally exercise power to our advantage. As I watch four- and five-year-old children play, and talk with them about it, I see constant struggles between them to make things happen that are to their own advantage. The struggle for power is infused through the very substance of their daily play, and is evident in:

- how children become included or excluded from play;
- which children have their play ideas taken up and used;
- who initiates play and how;
- who ends play and how;
- who uses what and when.

Read the following accounts of some of the children I observed and talked with, and think about the extent to which power exists in their play.

Lucy and the power of the wand

Lucy has just managed to turn the climbing frame into a castle where no boys are allowed. She has used a magic wand to make them all vanish, and shouts at them, 'I've got the power, I've got the power!'

When I ask her what she means, she laughs and says, 'the power makes them go away'. Lucy's powerful magic wand has made the boys go away because the teacher has insisted whoever has the wand should have their wishes obeyed.

The boys are clear about two things: first, they won't get to have a turn unless they follow the rules; and second, the teacher is watching them closely to ensure that they do follow the rules.

Chloe and *Ghostbusters*

Chloe and three boys are tearing around the outside play area playing *Ghostbusters*. Chloe needs to keep telling the boys what to do next as they are not as familiar as she is with the storyline. After the fourth reminder from Chloe to the boys that they should be 'throwing a trap for the ghosts', the boys down their ghostbusting tools and leave. Chloe is crestfallen. She follows them and tries to convince them to play again. The boys refuse, saying she is 'too bossy'.

Talking with the boys about this episode, they explained at length that boys should be the bosses and that they were bored with Chloe always bossing. Bosses, explained Charles, 'make people do things' and 'boys like being bosses'. Another boy, William, complained that 'she was bossy to me she pulled me and dragged me around the place'. Chloe strongly denied William's assessment of her managerial approach!

John and the birthday party

John is listening to Sarah invite several girls to her birthday party. The girls are seated in a boat in the outside play area, swapping treats with Sarah to try and secure an invitation to her birthday party. Offers of forbidden lollies and promises to let Sarah play with a newly acquired Barbie doll hidden in one girl's locker seem the most successful strategies for gaining an invite.

John moves closer and asks if he can come too. He offers Sarah a play with his new gun. She is not impressed, and says he can't come. After trying several other toys, he says that he 'hates her party anyway', and starts chanting a rhyme at her and the other girls. The rhyme is, 'Girls are sexy just like Pepsi!'. He keeps chanting it until Sarah starts to cry. At this point John says to Sarah that he'd stop if he can come to her party.

In each of these experiences, children have either successfully made something happen that is to their advantage or are struggling to do so. Lucy enjoys having her own way on the climbing frame; the boys'

refusal to play *Ghostbusters* is a determined effort to be the bosses; and John's playful chant is a determined effort to make Sarah invite him to her party. These are neither unusual children nor unusual moments in children's play (Paley 1991). On the contrary, I would argue that they are remarkably ordinary children involved in remarkably ordinary play with each other. Playing for power is, in fact, a remarkably ordinary part of children's daily play—it is this that makes it dangerous.

Play is dangerous because there is so much at stake. It is through play that children construct their understandings of the social world in which they live and learn to value themselves and others (Fleer 1996). Through play, they can construct play worlds in which they practise and learn to be fair, to share power, and to enjoy social diversity (Derman-Sparks 1993–4; Neugebauer 1992; Kyoung & Lewis 1995). Equally, however, it is through play that children can construct play worlds in which they practise and learn to be unfair, to compete for power, and to fear social diversity. They can create and experience racism, sexism, homophobia and classism (Derman-Sparks 1993–4; Creaser & Dau 1995).

We know from research in Australia and overseas that children can and do create such inequalities in their play worlds (Alloway 1995; MacNaughton 1996). They practise what they learn from each other and the adult world about gender, sexuality, love, hate, power, violence, friendship, inclusion and exclusion—and because of this, play can be dangerous for many children. It can be a place where others hurt you, call you names, ignore your ideas and exclude you. When girls play with many boys, when children of one ethnic group play with those of another, when working-class children play with middle-class children, or when children with disabilities play with children without disabilities, play can be risky. It can place you at risk of being hurt, being called names, having your ideas ignored or being ignored yourself. Children know this, as illustrated by these comments of several four-year-olds about their own play worlds:

- 'Being black is hard work.' (Brown 1995, p. 13)
- 'Boys and girls are on different teams, that's why they don't play together.'
- 'I don't like being a boy, they hurt girls too much.'
- 'I feel sad when they say I can't have two mummies.'

Much evidence in recent years shows that children quickly learn who has power, and the risk of playing with others when they don't have it because of who they are (Derman-Sparks 1993–4; Creaser & Dau 1995; Siraj-Blatchford 1994). One group of children is particularly prone to these risks; that is, those who choose to cross traditional gender boundaries in and through their play.

Playing across the gender boundaries

Girls who choose to cross traditional gender boundaries in their play often:

- try to play with the more traditional boys in the group;
- want to play the latest superhero;
- are noisier and more physically active than most other girls.

Often they wear 'unisex' clothes, have short hair and, in addition to being active, are articulate and confident.

Boys who choose to cross traditional gender boundaries in their play often:

- try to play with the more traditional girls in the group;
- want to join in domestic play;
- are quieter and less physically active than many of the other boys;
- wear traditional clothes, have longish hair, and are gentle and shy, yet articulate.

The consequences for boys and girls who cross the traditional gender boundaries in their pretend play can differ. However, both tend to experience frustration, rejection and often isolation in their pretend play as they try out what it means to 'do gender' differently. The experiences of Chloe clearly illustrate this.

Introducing Chloe

When I first met Chloe late in kindergarten she was nearly five years old. It was clear from our first meeting that she was not a traditionally 'feminine' girl, even in appearance. She always wore pants or shorts to kindergarten, and by November was beginning to resist the idea that she would need to wear a dress as part of her school uniform the following year. She had short, straight, blond hair, a strong body and a loud voice. The difference in her physical appearance compared to that of many of the other girls in the group was marked. Several girls had long curly hair, pink bows, pretty floral and lace dresses and patent leather shoes.

Chloe's personal style was also different. She was an extremely sociable, talkative and active child, whereas most of the other girls had a quiet and gentle manner. It was clear from watching her that she loved pretend play full of adventure and detailed storylines, while the majority of other girls preferred pretend play based on domestic storylines.

Chloe and the boys

On the surface, Chloe's seemed a major non-sexist success story. She was regularly involved in pretend play with the boys in which adventure storylines predominated. *Ghostbusters* and *Ninja Turtles* provided her with many of her favourite ones, which often required her to run around the outside play area, scramble to the top of the climbing frame, shout orders to the boys, engage in rough and tumble fights, and capture groups of 'baddies'. She described to me one such segment of pretend *Ghostbusters* play, which I had videotaped, as follows:

> *Chloe* (pointing to the video screen): Oh, there's me!
> *Glenda*: Do you know what game you were playing?
> *Chloe*: Ghostbusters.
> *Glenda*: Can you tell me about the game? What things do you do in the game?
> *Chloe*: Yeah, okay. See, they're the guys that catch the ghosts and one time when they were doing it at the bowling hall there was a big fight. Then they catch the ghosts and they throw the trap one day when they go shooting . . . and they come down, then they go to this trap.

Chloe clearly relished such play but it was not without its difficulties for her. As illustrated earlier, the boys with whom she regularly played, such as Charles and William, often left her when they thought she was being too 'bossy'. Chloe would then be caught between two contradictory desires—she wanted to be the boss, but she also wanted to continue playing with the boys. Her desire to be boss came from a sense of what she could accomplish:

> *Glenda*: Now you're the boss in this game. Do you like being the boss?
> *Chloe*: Yeah!
> *Glenda*: What do you get to do when you're the boss?
> *Chloe*: You get to do a lot of things, see. If you want to get something right, you have got to do it yourself.

Her desire to continue to play with the boys came from knowing that play with the girls would involve definite limits on what she could do:

> *Glenda*: Do you ever play in the home corner with the girls, Chloe?
> *Chloe*: You mean when someone is the mum?
> *Glenda*: What do the boys play in those games?
> *Chloe*: They play going to work, or anything that's real important, yeah.
> *Glenda*: Girls can do more things, but they play mum.

By contrast, play with the boys involved playing in what she called 'the real game', and for good reason—in 'the real game' she was always 'the only girl':

> *Glenda*: You're a girl playing with the boys. Do you play with the boys lots?
> *Chloe*: Yeah, I normally do 'cos boys are really in the real game. There was only one girl. I couldn't do anything else. (short break) In the real film it was the boys. There's only one girl. I couldn't do anything else.
> *Glenda*: Can you tell me more about playing with the boys?
> *Chloe*: Oh, yeah okay. You see the thing is (pause) boys . . . (fades) There were only boys in the whole movie and there's many more boys in other movies than girls. There's normally just one girl and more boys.

Chloe's sense of how the 'real game' worked came from video and television. Her world of video and television told her that action-based adventures were the province of the boys. The space for girls within them was limited: one girl per adventure film. This understanding helped her make sense of why she was often the only girl playing with the boys in her pretend play. It also allowed her to think that being the only girl in boys' play was a reasonable and recognisable way to 'do' her gender.

However, being 'only one girl' in the 'real game' also had considerable drawbacks. These are powerfully illustrated in the segment of pretend play that follows.

Chloe and the pink tent

Chloe had been playing in the outside play area under a metal A-frame over which two pink blankets had been draped. Chloe had called it her 'house' during a game of mothers and sisters with three other girls. The game had not lasted very long as two boys (John and Andrew) came over and tried to enter her house. Chloe defended it with loud shouts of, 'Get out of my tent!' At this point, the boys left and so did the girls.

Chloe decides that her tent would make a good shop and, with the teacher's help, gathers a wicker basket full of empty packages to 'sell'. Chloe returns with her basket.

Andrew (moving over): I can't have any, can I?

Chloe: If you want to pay for it, you can. Here's your food (she hands him a box and Andrew leaves).

Chloe is by herself again and she tells me she will have to 'just yell out' to let the children know she has some food for sale. However, before she can do so, Andrew and John reappear and take two boxes from her basket without asking. Chloe yells at them, 'Don't! You don't have to steal. Don't! Don't! They are stealing my things.'

The boys leave again. Chloe is alone again, so begins to shout, 'I'm selling fruit if you can pay. I'm selling fruit!' For two minutes she waits and watches and then starts again: 'Fruit for sale, fruit for sale, fruit for sale!'

Andrew and John return and this time pick up two boxes and try to pull them apart. Chloe looks distressed and they quickly move to the back of the tent and start climbing on it. They are joined by three other boys and begin calling themselves robbers. They tell Chloe they are going to rob her shop.

Chloe: They are bothering me. Go away. Get out!

One of the boys throws a box at Chloe and the others are pushing up, over and through the tent. They are making 'monster' noises and laughing. This continues for a while.

Chloe: Bye, bye. That's all you know. The shop is closed.

The boys continue climbing all over the shop and start saying things it is difficult to hear.

Chloe (shouting): That's not very nice. They said 'disgusting idiot'. James did. I'm not going to invite you to my birthday party!

James (calling): Open up your house. I'm the police!

Chloe: This is not a police station. There's the police station! (pointing to a nearby covered playhouse)

The boys move to the police station.

Chloe: Here's your pie and sausage roll from the shop.

She takes them lunch (a couple of boxes). They eat for a moment and then begin to move all over the tent again. Chloe looks at me, puts her hand in the air and says, 'What's a girl got to do around here?' She eventually decides to try to sell her house but finds that no one wants to buy it.

Crossing the gender boundaries for Chloe meant facing daily dilemmas as she tried to satisfy her desire to be in the 'real game' and to 'do more things' than 'play mum'. As this story illustrates, there are limits placed on being a girl in a boys' world, and a girl can only go so far before these limits are imposed. In this case, Chloe's setting up shop and running it was allowed to the point the boys enforced their limits on her. Like women entering the male corporate world, girls crossing the gender boundaries in pretend play have 'glass ceilings' imposed on how far they can go in the boys' world.

This imposing of limits happens through a constant power battle that is often begun the moment a girl creates and attempts to maintain a powerful position in the boys' play world. For girls who successfully negotiate this power battle with boys, their pleasure can be considerable. However, it is easy for such success to be short-lived as the power battle rarely lasts. For Chloe, each twist and turn in which she tried to gain back her control was met with resistance. Hence, for girls wanting to cross the gender boundaries, pretend play is full of dilemmas: whether to enter the battle, whether to give it up, and whether to subvert it.

Chloe's experiences highlight how these pretend play dilemmas look in practice. In the episode of the pink tent, Chloe found herself constantly negotiating power relations with the boys and facing the dilemma: to battle to be boss, or not. This dilemma arose from the pleasures but also the dangers she associated with being boss.

The pleasures of being boss included:

- experiencing the joy of getting 'to do a lot of things';
- getting something right because 'you have got to do it yourself';
- being in the 'real game';
- being like the women in the movies through being 'just one girl'.

The dangers in being boss included risking:

- physical and sometimes violent harassment by the boys;
- the boys leaving and thus being left to play by herself;
- having her storyline subverted by the boys;
- the boys' resistance to her power as the boss.

Being boss, to Chloe, meant potential pleasures, but also facing the reality that her pink tent had a 'glass ceiling'; not being boss removed her potential pleasures, but reduced the dangers of being 'kept down', 'kept out' or 'kept away' by the boys. Crossing the traditional gender boundaries in pretend play meant that Chloe faced the pleasures and dangers of her gender choices on a daily basis. The 'glass ceiling' in her pink tent regularly found its way into the other pretend play spaces and storylines she engaged in with the boys. As a result, her pretend play life was often problematic, frustrating and isolating—as well as exciting, challenging and fun. She explored, experienced and maintained her difference from the other girls at a cost and at considerable risk to her relations with the boys.

Talking with Chloe and watching what she risked through her pretend play it was easy to see why so many girls avoid 'doing' their gender differently to the norm. It was also easy to see that Chloe's understanding of who she was as a girl consisted of a complex web of views and understandings in which pleasure and danger regularly surfaced. As long as she continued to 'do' gender differently and to cross the boundaries created and maintained by other children in the group, Chloe would face the daily dilemma of whether or not she should try to break through the 'glass ceiling'. Further, she would need to live with the possibility that her attempts to do so would frequently result in frustration and possible isolation.

The challenge for early childhood staff working with children like Chloe is twofold. They have to:

- develop strategies to minimise the risks they encounter when they reach for and try to break through the 'glass ceiling' imposed by others in the play world;

- help them to understand, be proud of, and committed to, their difference.

Minimising the risks of crossing the gender boundaries

Once staff are alert to the potential risks for those children who choose to cross the gender boundaries, they can work to minimise them. There are six simple ways in which staff can do this.

Six-point risk-minimisation plan

1. **Be alert**—regularly observe the power dynamics in children's pretend play (for in-depth information, see MacNaughton 1995[b]).
2. **Be explorative**—encourage the children to talk about (objectify) their play experiences to clarify how they feel about what is happening. Create opportunities to explore their feelings about gender through informal discussions, stories, song, movement and art.
3. **Be honest**—talk with the children about gender differences in ways that recognise the difficulty involved in being different. For instance, be open about the disadvantages as well as the advantages of being strong, caring and so on.
4. **Be 'promotional'**—find female heroines and male heroes that have crossed the gender boundaries, and share stories, songs, poems and images with the children that promote different ways of being as acceptable.
5. **Be provocative**—provoke discussion with the children about the fact that people have different ideas about gender.
6. **Be supportive**—talk with the children about the ways in which we each feel 'different' sometimes. Make it 'okay' for them to have 'contradictory' ways of being at times, and discuss the fun of trying out being different kinds of people.

The value of pretend play

Reading this account of children's pretend play, some may think that it is not children's play that is dangerous but this analysis of it. To claim that children's play is about power and is often dangerous is, perhaps, provocative. We have a long tradition of valuing children's play and arguing that it is the cornerstone of a distinctive and important approach to early childhood education (Fleer 1996). Feeney, Christenson and Moravcik, for example, talk of play as the 'ultimate realisation of the early childhood educator's maxim of learning by doing' (Feeney, Christenson & Moravcik 1991, p. 100). Similarly, Hildebrand lists 16 values of play, claiming that it is valuable because it:

- aids growth;
- is a voluntary activity;
- offers a child freedom of action;
- provides an imaginary world that a child can master;
- contains elements of adventure;
- provides a base for learning language;
- has unique power for building interpersonal relationships;
- offers opportunities for mastery of the physical self;
- furthers interest and concentration;
- enables a child to investigate the material world;
- is a way of learning adult roles;
- is always a dynamic way of learning;
- refines a child's judgment;
- can be academically structured;
- is vitalising;
- is essential to the survival of human beings.

(Based on Hildebrand 1991, p. 50)

Since there is evidence that play can do all these things, surely we should value it as an early childhood developmental experience? Certainly we want to appreciate the positive side of play and encourage it to build up children's various skills but, in my view, our validation of play is problematic because it is uncritical. As shown in this chapter, play is not always positive, nor necessarily valuable. What children can gain from play is highly conditional and depends on who they are, who they are playing with, how they are playing with each other, what they are playing and what happens during the day. In fact, play can accomplish precisely the opposite of what Hildebrand (1991) claims, as the following situations demonstrate:

- When a white child says to a black child, 'you can't play here 'cos your skin is dirty', play restricts, rather than enhances, a child's freedom of action.
- When girls constantly learn storylines in which only males can be active and powerful leaders, play can make girls feel disempowered rather than empowered.

- When a boy loves playing mum or cuddling babies but no-one else wants to play with him, play can be boring rather than exciting.
- When a girl has a speech disability and others laugh at or ignore her when she speaks, play can reduce rather than broaden her opportunity to develop language.
- When someone stands on the climbing frame and shouts, 'no bloody wogs here', play can restrict children's attempts to be physically active rather than encourage them.
- When a girl who loves playing with blocks regularly gets them knocked over by the boys when the teacher is not looking, she loses interest in blocks and instead concentrates on where the boys and teachers are. Is this what we want her to concentrate on?
- When a group of boys are excited by their game of digging for treasure in the sandpit, it can be dispiriting rather than vitalising for the girls playing in the same area to be showered by sand.

The value of play cannot be separated from what is being learnt through it. For instance:

- When play is a way of reinforcing traditional genders in adult roles, is it valuable?
- When play is a dynamic way of learning that boys won't play with confident, physically active girls, is it valuable?
- When play reinforces a child's judgment that it is silly to be caring if you are a boy, is it valuable?

The value of play cannot be divorced from its social context and social implications. Unless we check how and in whose interests power is being exercised during play, we cannot know what its social, and hence developmental, implications might be. We cannot know for whom play is dangerous and for whom it is safe.

Conclusion

As staff observe children's pretend play, I believe they need to think about what can be gained and learnt by seeing power and danger in children's play. I would argue that if we don't see it, we are in danger of condoning the inequalities and injustices that children so effectively construct in their daily play. We must acknowledge the power and danger in play in order to work with children to construct a more equitable world in the present and future. We have to see something before we can decide what to do about it and how to change it.

Seeing the power and danger in children's play, we must decide how to use play to make early childhood education more fair and safe for all children, then use our power to help achieve this. Children cannot make play fair and safe by themselves—we, as adults, need to intervene to help them learn how to be respectful of diversity. It is from adults that children learn how to play for power and how to make play dangerous; it is from adults that they must un-learn this and revisit play anew.

At a time when intolerance is gaining some ground worldwide, we need to be vigilant as to how children reconstruct these visions in their play. To this end, I would urge you to keep in mind the words of Kathleen McGinnis: 'To raise children who will champion justice, they must first experience justice.' (Hashimoto 1996)

Play cannot and should not be valued unless it is equitable and safe for all involved. For boys and girls who choose to cross the traditional gender boundaries, such fairness and safety cannot yet be assumed. Staff must actively participate with children at play to create a fairer and safer world.

For further thought and discussion

1. To what extent do you agree with the idea that the struggle for power is infused through the very substance of children's daily play?
2. Observe an episode of children's pretend play that lasts for at least 20 minutes. Comment on the following:

   • How were children included or excluded from play?
   • Which children had their play ideas taken up and used?
   • Who initiated play and how?
   • Who ended play and how?
   • Who ended up using what, and when?
3. Observe a group of four- and five-year-old children. Which ones are crossing the gender boundaries? How do you know this? To what extent are they having positive experiences in crossing the gender boundaries?
4. Review the six-point risk-minimisation plan for children crossing the gender boundaries. Would you modify it in any way if you were working with children under three years old?
5. What are some questions you could use to help you understand how the children who cross the gender boundaries feel about what they are doing?

6. Review a selection of children's picture books. How many books can you find that show heroines and heroes crossing the gender boundaries?
7. Write your own story showing a male or female successfully crossing the gender boundaries.
8. Identify three ways in which you could support both boys and girls attempting to cross the gender boundaries. Would the age of the children make any difference to the strategies you decide to use?

References

Alloway, N. 1995, *Foundation Stones: The Construction of Gender in Early Childhood*, Curriculum Corporation, Melbourne.

Brown, B. 1995, *All our Children: A Guide for those who Care*, BBC Books, London.

Creaser, B. & Dau, E. (eds) 1995, *The Anti-Bias Approach in Early Childhood*, Harper-Educational, Sydney.

Danby, S. 1996, Rites of passage: masculinity in the block area, paper presented to the Reconceptualizing Early Childhood Education: Research, Theory and Practice, Sixth Annual Interdisciplinary Conference, Madison, Wisconsin, 10–12 Oct.

Davies, B. 1989, *Frogs and Snails and Feminist Tales*, Allen & Unwin, Sydney.

Derman-Sparks, L. & the Anti-Bias Task Force 1989, *Anti-Bias Curriculum: Tools for Empowering Young Children*, National Association for the Education of Young Children, Washington DC.

Derman-Sparks, L. 1993–4, 'Empowering children to create a caring culture in a world of difference', *Childhood Education*, vol. 70(2), pp. 66–71.

Feeney, S., Christenson, D. & Moravcik, E. 1991, 4th edn, *Who am I in the Lives of Children? An Introduction to Teaching Young Children*, Macmillan Publishing Company, New York.

Fleer, M. (ed.) 1996, *Play through the Profiles: Profiles through Play*, Australian Early Childhood Association, Canberra.

Grieshaber, S. 1996, Beating mum: how to win the power game, paper presented to the Reconceptualizing Early Childhood Education: Research, Theory and Practice, Sixth Annual Interdisciplinary Conference, Madison, Wisconsin. October 10–12.

Hashimoto, R. 1996, 'Some quotes to ponder and enjoy', *The Web Journal of the Culturally Relevant Anti-Bias Early Childhood Educators' Network*, vol. 11(1), p. 27.

Hildebrand, V. 1991, 5th edn, *Introduction to Early Childhood Education*, Macmillan Publishing Company, New York.

Kyoung, K. & Lewis, G. 1995, The effect of gender role stereotyping of Asian–Australian and Australian preschool children of an anti-bias curriculum, paper presented to the conference Tolerance and Beyond, Woden, ACT, 21–22 Apr.

MacNaughton, G. 1995(a), 'A poststructuralist analysis of learning in early childhood settings', in *DAPcentrism: Challenging Developmentally Appropriate Practice*, Fleer, M. (ed.), Australian Early Childhood Association, Canberra.

MacNaughton, G. 1995(b), 'The gender factor', in *The Anti-Bias Approach in Early Childhood*, Creaser, B. & Dau, E. (eds), HarperEducational, Sydney.

MacNaughton, G. 1996, 'Girls, boys and race: where's the power?', *The Web Journal of the Culturally Relevant Anti-Bias Early Childhood Educators' Network*, vol. 11(1), pp. 1–17.

Miller, J. 1993, *The Passion of Michel Foucault*, Flamingo Press, London.

Neugebauer, B. (ed.) 1992, *Alike and Different: Exploring Our Humanity with Young Children*, National Association for the Education of Young Children, Washington DC.

Paley, V. 1991, *Bad Guys don't have Birthdays: Fantasy Play at Four*, University of Chicago Press, Chicago.

Siraj-Blatchford, I. 1994, *Laying the Foundations for Racial Inequity in the Early Years*, Trentham Books, London.

Walkerdine, V. 1981, 'Sex, power and pedagogy', *Screen*, vol. 38, pp. 14–24.

Chapter 8

Play and the gifted child

Cathie Harrison and Kim Tegel

Introduction

Giftedness is a significant aspect of human diversity that is evident in early childhood. Research indicates that giftedness is both inherited and acquired, and a reality for infants, toddlers and young children, as well as their families and caregivers (Clark 1992; Piechowski & Colangelo 1984). Young children who are gifted require education and care which nourishes and fosters their uniqueness and supports the many aspects of childhood that they share with all children. To reach their full potential, they must be provided with experiences and interactions that are responsive to their advanced development and particular characteristics.

For young children who are gifted, play is a precious and valuable experience. The context of free and spontaneous play can be the source of powerful learning and personal satisfaction. In play, the child is free to initiate, direct, complicate and pursue an interest to a point of personal resolution. For the gifted child, this play may be far more involved and complex than that typical of most children their age. Gifted children can also explore and 'play out' some of the social, emotional and moral issues which fascinate and perplex them.

At school I feel like I'm in a big boundary. I can't get to find out about the things I want to find out about. When I'm playing I have more time, more time for just one thing, instead of doing five things at once: spelling, maths, story-writing, up-and-down sums and reading. At school they tell you before you get to find out for yourself in your own way. When you are playing it's different because you get to ask all your own questions and find out for yourself in just the way that you want to.

(Comments of a gifted child aged six)

Unfortunately for the gifted child, such play is often considered a waste of time by adults, and periods of free play are replaced with structured activities and academic tasks. However, free and self-directed play provides one of the most effective contexts which adults can provide to meet the socio-emotional and learning needs of the gifted child (Harrison 1995; Parke & Ness 1988; Tegel 1992; Wright 1990).

Characteristics of the gifted child

Gifted children are a diverse group and it is important to recognise that there is no typical gifted child. Giftedness may be demonstrated in a range of ways (Tegel 1994) and may or may not be evident across all developmental areas. Characteristics of the young child who is gifted may include:

- advanced physical development;
- intensity of purpose;
- curiosity;
- exceptional memory;
- rapid pace of learning;
- early reading skills;
- asking probing questions;
- advanced mathematical ability;
- creativity and imagination;
- sense of humour;
- ability to generalise knowledge and apply it to new situations;
- being articulate and expressive with an extensive vocabulary;
- offering alternative and divergent solutions to problems;
- ability to follow complex instructions;
- wide range of interests;
- advanced social interactions;
- heightened sensitivity;
- social maturity;
- differences in play patterns;
- perfectionism;
- resisting unfairness and having a strong sense of social justice;
- questioning authority;
- being perceptive regarding the feelings of others.

(Based on Ehrlich 1985; Gross 1993; Harrison 1995; Silverman 1993)

Play patterns of the gifted child

The characteristics of giftedness outlined above have a significant influence on the way young children who are gifted play with others and with resources. Research by Barnett and Fiscella (1985, cited in Harrison 1995) indicates that the play of gifted children tends to be developmentally advanced, often resembling the play patterns of older children of average intelligence. They suggest that, in general, gifted children prefer the company of older playmates and demonstrate more advanced play styles, use higher levels of imagination and creative playful interactions. They are also more pro-social in their play, acting more cooperatively and exhibiting more sharing behaviour than their peers.

Social maturity and high levels of imagination and creativity can result in a range of responses and play behaviours in gifted children. Some become frustrated by their differences from their peers and vent their feelings in aggressive or destructive behaviour, while some seek out like-minded peers or more mature companions in the form of older children and/or adults. For others, solitary play provides the most satisfying play experience and this can result in social isolation that may be perceived as introversion.

While this perception may be common, it is important to note that introversion has been defined as a basic personality trait in which individuals gain energy from being alone rather than, as with extroverts, being with others. As Silverman says, 'introverts feel drained by too much association with others: they need to retreat from the world to regain their sense of balance' (Silverman 1988, in Whitmore 1986, p. 82). Such personality differences need to be respected if each child is to develop a positive self-concept. Differences in play patterns need to be supported with a variety of shared and solitary experiences. Valuable play experiences can occur without observable interaction with other people.

Often one of the prime objectives for offering play experiences to young children is to assist in the processes of their social development. Social development involves a sense of self-acceptance that comes from positive interaction with others, regardless of age, and for many young gifted children this may well be with an adult. As Silverman observes: 'Lasting friendships are based on mutual interests and values, not on age. Individuals with good social development like themselves, like other people, demonstrate concern for humanity and develop mutually rewarding friendships with a few kindred spirits.' (Silverman 1992, p. 15)

Characteristics such as commitment to a particular task, curiosity, an unusually long attention span and ability to understand and use abstract concepts may also impact on the nature of the play of the gifted child. Such children may pursue interests that are unusual in early childhood. For example, although most children in early childhood demonstrate play themes and interests which are based on the familiar and the concrete, it is often the abstract and unfamiliar which preoccupies the gifted child. For gifted children, interests and play themes can include such diverse aspects as ecological issues, astronomy, ancient civilisations and cultures, current political and sociological issues and moral dilemmas. Such interests are often pursued through various forms of play with an intensity, creativity and complexity which may surprise adults.

Amanda, Sabine and Said, all aged four, were playing in the family corner. They began to play out the roles involved in food preparation using the plastic food available.

Sabine: This stuff is no good for babies. It's too big and they won't be able to digest it. We need mushy stuff.

Amanda: We don't have any mushy stuff.

Sabine: Well, the babies will die then—you know—malnutrition like the babies in those countries where there isn't enough food. They get big tummies but they aren't fat. You know those ones in Africa when it doesn't rain or where there's a war . . . and they can't go to the shops.

Said (listening intently): Let's play that then. You know, where they go out looking to find food. We could go and dig in the sandpit and pick some leaves and get sticks.

Sabine (enthusiastically): Yeah, let's do that—and we could mash up some sand and some leaves and then feed them and they wouldn't die.

The three children left the family corner to continue their play that involved foraging for food. Their play was accompanied by much complex conversation about the difficulties of survival in the third world.

This play scenario was repeated with variations in the outdoor environment over several weeks. The same three children also collaborated in the task of building a shelter with sheets and mats under the trees.

Play: a context for learning

Young children who are gifted gain much from opportunities to engage in rich and complex play experiences (Harrison 1995; Tegel 1994; Wright 1990). Adults should be aware of some of the important aspects of play for these children and plan for opportunities like the following:

1. Participating in experiences which use executive operations, such as forecasting or predicting, hypothesising, planning, decision making, communicating and evaluating (Kitano 1982). Critical and flexible thinking is developed when children evaluate and make decisions regarding issues and occurrences in their play. In this approach, it is the processes rather than a particular outcome or product which is considered significant, and trial and error learning is legitimised. In play, mistakes can be perceived as learning experiences; that is, as alternative pathways or directions rather than errors of which to be ashamed. This is particularly important for the child who is gifted and demonstrates a tendency towards perfectionism.

Tracey and Sam, Joanna and Tan gathered the sheets and blankets from the family corner. They asked to borrow the rugs used at fruit time and disappeared down to the back corner of the playground. After 20 minutes, it was obvious that the children had been working well together. Several of the rugs were suspended from low branches of the tree to form walls, and another was spread between two branches as a makeshift roof. The windy conditions had demanded particular resourcefulness, problem solving and collaboration. The children had used the pegs from the painting area and skipping ropes from the outdoor shed to secure the rugs. Some old tyres from the climbing area served the dual purpose of anchoring the floor and functioning as furniture, such as baths and beds. When asked to explain the play to the adults and other children, the four children gave a long and detailed explanation of the various steps and stages in their construction.

---

2. Playing out and following through the events they have experienced, stories they have read or unfamiliar concepts of which they have become aware.
3. Participating in the processes of research and documentation.

> Emma, aged three, was playing and painting with water on the path. She noticed that the water disappeared all by itself and asked, 'Where has it gone? How can it just disappear?' The adult responded, 'Yes, it's gone. I wonder where it has gone to? Do you think that it disappears when we paint in the shade? What about when we spill water on the floor inside? Does it disappear by itself too? Let's go and paint in some other places and see what happens.' Other questions included, 'What happens to the water in the washing when we hang it out to dry? What happens to the puddles left after the rain?'

The adult supported Emma's thinking and discovery by responding positively to her sense of wonder and by encouraging her to participate actively in exploring this interest.

Since young children who are gifted are capable of acquiring knowledge more easily than their peers, they require less time to master routine tasks. They also benefit from being able to take responsibility for their own learning (Karnes, Schwedel & Williams 1983). Play facilitates this, because it encourages children to pursue their interests and allows for their differing levels of ability. Play environments can be pre-planned by the early childhood educator to help develop the child's individual strengths and needs.

The role of the supportive adult

Engaging children

Play supported by a sensitive and observant adult provides an excellent forum for gifted children to develop their character and particular interests or skills. Adults need to adopt strategies that will engage children in processes to help them achieve this. These strategies could include involving the child in planning the play environment, selecting resources, organising group projects and sharing information with others. Young children who are gifted can use advanced language, literacy, numeracy and/or research skills in this process.

Adults need to ask open-ended questions which focus on the how and why.

Olivia, aged three and a half, found a measuring tape in the garage. 'What's this?' she asked her mother. Her mother responded, 'It's a measuring tape. You can have a look at it. Have you seen one of these before?' Olivia shook her head. 'Well, have a play with it. See what's written on it? How do you think that you could use it? Why don't you take it outside and play with it and see how it works?' Olivia returned after about 15 minutes. She spoke quickly and excitedly: 'I need one of these at preschool. I need it to know which one of the children is the biggest and which is the littlest. I need it when we are building with blocks so we know who has the longest road. I need one too!'

In such situations the direction is determined by the child and the particular solution reached by the child is personally meaningful and does not need to be evaluated by the adult.

The posing of additional questions by the adult can engage the child in research by encouraging him or her to draw on previous observations, knowledge and understanding to focus on a new dilemma. Rather than answering a question directly, the adult 'scaffolds' for the child, enabling the child to reach a new point of understanding. Adult and child can engage in co-construction of knowledge. Together they share the play with ideas as well as resources and participate in further research and investigation.

The adult needs to be sensitive to opportunities for:

- formulating and testing new hypotheses;
- experimenting and researching through books;
- accessing experts.

These opportunities give gifted children greater understanding of the initial puzzling question, as well as assisting them to develop autonomy in research. This is invaluable not only because it empowers the child to become an independent learner, but also because it alleviates some of the pressure on educators and families to satisfy the insatiable need for new information often demonstrated by gifted children.

Resourcing children's play

Access to additional resources is necessary in children's play, as is the presence of an adult open to those resources being used in new and unexpected ways. Access to open-ended resources can facilitate the child's participation in satisfying play experiences. Play resources, such as blocks and dress-ups, have infinite possibilities for complex and creative use. The creative possibilities such resources offer—and the varying degrees of complexity of play which can be attained with them—are determined by the child, who will find them personally satisfying as well as challenging.

Early readers can soon learn to access indexes and catalogues, phone books, dictionaries, maps, directories and encyclopaedias, while the adult can act as a mentor or guide. It is important, however, to allow the child to take the lead and to be responsive to the child's thinking. Adults who adopt this role should not be inhibited or constrained by expectations of a child's typical interests or levels of understanding. Young children who are gifted frequently pursue interests in great depth and complexity and often contemplate issues not generally considered in the early childhood curriculum. They often have high levels of task commitment, curiosity and persistence. If gifted children are to retain their intrinsic motivation and curiosity, the ideas and issues that are self-generated must be acknowledged and responded to regardless of their complexity.

Exploring complex issues

Young children who are gifted are able to demonstrate a heightened sense of social justice, and frequently demonstrate intense emotional sensitivity towards their own feelings and those of others (Harrison 1995; Kitano 1982). They therefore need opportunities to play out feelings, reflect on situations of concern and pursue moral dilemmas to complex levels. During play, children can enact a moral dilemma and then develop a number of responses to it. Tegel (1992) suggests that in play children can repeat experiences and scenarios and so take as much time as they need to express and come to terms with feelings, interests and everyday experiences as well as unfamiliar, perplexing and even fearful events.

In addition, adults can guide and support the child's thinking in contemplating issues of concern. They can empathise with the feelings which the play may generate and encourage alternative and creative responses.

> George, aged four, found block play very frustrating. He wanted to build complex structures that required the use of many blocks. He became very angry when he saw other children, as he said, 'wasting blocks just making long straight roads.' The adults, who wished to support the play of all children in the centre, spent considerable time observing the block play area. They discussed the incidents in the block area with the children thoughtfully, and all together worked out particular strategies to solve the problem. This experience provided George with the opportunity to verbalise his feelings, use his creative problem-solving abilities and help him understand the perspective of others.

Connections with like-minded peers

Young children who are gifted require opportunities to connect with like-minded peers. Koopmans-Dayton & Feldhusen (1987) support this notion as does Harrison (1995) who further suggests that mixed age grouping increases opportunities for peer cooperation, while also responding to individual needs. Play offers this opportunity because children with similar interests can play together, regardless of age. Play also allows children to participate as they wish and to take the play to a level of complexity which suits them. This suggests, then, that children may play together at the same play experience, but the play which takes place may vary depending upon each child's interests and the level of complexity satisfying to that child.

Time for play

Gifted children may require longer periods of uninterrupted time and the opportunity to revisit an experience over several days, weeks or months before they can explore an interest or concern to a point of resolution and personal completion. It is important that the child has the opportunity to determine this point of closure rather than having it imposed by the adult. Frequently, adults inform children that an experience is finished, saying such things as, 'you have done enough of that now—come and do something else', rather than allowing the children to determine this for themselves. Gifted children may respond to this with an emotional outburst that can be surprising to the adult!

Characteristics of giftedness such as intense feelings, heightened sensitivity and perfectionism may manifest themselves in this situation, so a sensitive and supportive response is required from the adult. The ability to empathise with the child is significant. For instance, the adult may comment, 'I know that you're not finished yet and it must be difficult to have to pack away.' This acknowledges the child's feelings and legitimises them. The adult may then offer the child an opportunity to think of alternative solutions to the dilemma, which in turn helps the child to identify and manage the problem. Reminders of pack-away time and opportunities to revisit the experience by taking photographs of the play process and products or videotaping them can help the child to feel more comfortable about the transient nature of much play.

Opportunities for creativity

Young children who are gifted also require adults to implement strategies that will support the use and further development of their creativity. Free play with open-ended resources can provide opportunities in which adults can encourage a range of creative processes such as:

- fluency—the ability to give many different responses;
- flexibility—the ability to change perspective;
- originality—the ability to produce unique responses;
- embellishment—the ability to develop or add detail. (Torrance 1969)

Socio-dramatic play—such as that using blocks, sand and water, construction materials, paints, paper and clay—provides infinite opportunities for the child to develop these processes. Adults can facilitate creative and divergent thinking in children by observing, listening and extending their play in numerous ways.

First, they can give young children the opportunity to play and explore things in a safe atmosphere; that is, provide a context which encourages unusual and unique responses on the part of the children, which acknowledges and is supportive of differences rather than conformity, and which supports risk-taking. The imaginative use of resources and the provision of uninterrupted and extended playing time is fundamental. Open-ended resources again play a vital part. Visual art experiences such as collage, drawing, painting and work with clay are excellent ways to assist the development of these thinking skills.

Second, adults can enhance opportunities to develop creative thinking by giving encouragement and affirmation to the unusual and unexpected as, for example, with comments such as: 'That's an interesting idea. I have never thought of that before! What do you think will happen?' or 'Why?' or 'You could give it a try and see what happens. Let's watch carefully and see what happens and then we can talk about it and think about it further.'

Third, the adult can serve as a role model by demonstrating personal creativity and playfulness. Adults who show curiosity and a willingness to explore and investigate the unfamiliar can help empower the child. In the case of the gifted child who shows perfectionist tendencies, the opportunity to observe risk-taking, trial and error, failure and realistic self-evaluation is valuable. Adults who can admit that they make mistakes while learning, and that they do not know all the answers, offer a safe environment for the child to also make mistakes and ask unusual questions. Adult and child can then share in mutually satisfying investigation and discovery.

Complex language and advanced literacy and numeracy skills

Young children who are gifted need opportunities to use language in a variety of complex ways. Play allows children to experiment with language in rich and meaningful ways at a level that suits their needs and particular stage of development. Tegel (1992) further suggests that when children are involved in an experience, they often use words to describe it. Discussion can include a description of what they are doing and how they are feeling. The children learn from each other and have opportunities to use words that would not necessarily be needed or used in other experiences.

> Oona and Jye, both aged four, were playing with plastic cars in the sandpit. As Oona pushed her car through the sand it got stuck. Jye reached over, picked up the car and looked at it. He said: 'Well, if we could lift up the bonnet we could see if it's the radiator, or if it's the hoses, or the transmission. All sorts of things can go wrong with a car engine, you know.'

Young gifted children often learn to read at an earlier age than other children of the same age. The early reading ability and complex interests frequently demonstrated by gifted children should be supported by access to an appropriate range of literature. They need to have the opportunity to read fiction and factual texts which interest them and which are written to a level of complexity which satisfies them. Access to complete books, encyclopaedias and dictionaries as well as to publications such as manuals, catalogues and atlases can also be useful.

Literature and learning centres can be set up as part of a play environment in a non-structured and child-directed manner. Adults can assist by identifying children's interests through observing and listening to them and talking with their families. Resources relevant to a particular interest—such as books, objects, slides and videos—can then be accessed through public libraries and museums and through the support of families and the community. Children can also benefit greatly from opportunities to share their interests with an expert or someone who has a passionate interest in a similar topic. Such a person can act as a mentor and share the journey of discovery with the child.

Young children who are gifted need opportunities to use advanced skills of numeracy and literacy in meaningful contexts. These needs can be supported by access to literacy and numeracy resources in the context of play. Frequently children's first attempts at writing occur during play, where it is used for purposes that are relevant and significant to the children themselves. Play also offers opportunities for children to practice and develop numeracy skills in meaningful and appropriate ways. Resources often need to be shared with others, amounts calculated, measurements taken and sometimes, depending upon the nature of the play in which the children are involved, complex mathematical formulas developed, implemented, evaluated and then redeveloped.

Adults can support this process by offering relevant resources and 'scaffolding' to enable the child to reach a new understanding that may be beyond typical developmental expectations. Resources such as pencils, pads of paper, small writing books, chalk and chalkboards, beads, counters, buttons, calculators, computers, rulers, and measuring tapes can be helpful.

Conclusion

Adults who engage in the processes of supporting and participating in play with the gifted child develop a far greater understanding of the individual child. Play provides a window on children's development and the nature and depth of their thinking and feeling, and an insight into their interests and concerns. Such information is invaluable to both families and educators who seek to maximise positive learning opportunities for children. The information gathered by observing and documenting play provides an excellent basis for identification of giftedness. This information is also useful when planning a child-centred and responsive curriculum and when determining appropriate educational placements for the gifted child. Carefully documented examples of the child's learning through play can also help to explain the value of the child's play experiences to parents, families and others.

Children who are gifted, as all children, have a right to be affirmed and acknowledged for who they are. They, too, have a right to play. It is in play that young gifted children explore both their physical and social worlds. It is through their interaction with others in the context of play that such children begin to develop a sense of who they are as part of a community. In play, they learn to value themselves as unique individuals—individuals who are able to make a positive contribution to the world of which they are a part.

For further thought and discussion

1. What strategies could be used to assist a group of children to value and utilise the contributions of all children, including that of the gifted child?
2. In what ways can educators encourage families with gifted children to feel empowered and share in aspects of their child's development and home experiences?
3. How can the educator support gifted children and their families in the transition between child care services, preschools and school settings?
4. In what ways can the educator communicate the value of play for the gifted child to their families and other professionals?

References

Clark, B. 1992, 4th edn, *Growing up Gifted*, Macmillan, New York.
Ehrlich, V. 1985, *Gifted Children: A Guide for Parents and Teachers*, Trillium Press, New York.
Gross, M. 1993, *Exceptionally Gifted Children*, Routledge, London.
Harrison, C. 1995, *Giftedness in Early Childhood*, KU Children's Services, Sydney.

Karnes, M., Schwedel, A. & Williams, M. 1983, 'Combining instructional models for young gifted children', *Teaching Exceptional Children*, Spring, pp. 128–33.

Kitano, M. 1982, 'Young gifted children: strategies for preschool teachers', *Young Children*, May, pp. 14–23.

Koopmans-Dayton, J. & Feldhusen, J. 1987, 'A resource guide for the parents of gifted preschoolers', *Gifted Child Today*, Nov./Dec., pp. 2–7.

Parke, B. & Ness, P. 1988, 'Curricular decision-making for the education of young gifted children', *Gifted Child Quarterly*, vol. 32(1), pp. 196–9.

Piechowski, M. M. & Colangelo, N. 1994, 'Developmental potential of the gifted', *Gifted Child Quarterly*, vol. 28(20), pp. 80–88.

Silverman, L. 1992, 'Social development or socialisation?', *Understanding Our Gifted*, Sept./Oct., p. 15.

Silverman, L. 1993, *Counseling the Gifted*, Love Publishing Group, Denver, Colorado.

Tegel, K. 1992, 'Play', *Gifted* (72), pp. 9–10.

Tegel, K. 1994, 'Characteristics of very young gifted children', *Gifted*, (81), pp. 11–12.

Torrance, E. 1969, *Creativity*, Dimensions Publishing, Belmont, California.

Whitmore, J. (ed.) 1986, *Intellectual Giftedness in Young Children: Recognition and Development*, Haworth Press, New York.

Wright, L. 1990, 'The social and non-social behaviours of precocious pre-schoolers during freeplay' *Roeper Review*, 12(4), pp. 268–73.

Chapter 9

The place of play for young children with disabilities in mainstream education

Barbara Creaser

Main Editor's note

This paper was written following a workshop presentation given by Barbara at a conference organised by the Washington Association for the Education of Young Children. The royalties from this chapter will go to the Barbara Creaser Memorial Lecture Fund. Information about the Barbara Creaser Memorial Lecture precedes Chapter 3, 'Thinking about play, playing about thinking', written by Sue Dockett, the inaugural presenter of the lecture.

Readers will note that Barbara uses the term 'teacher'. Barbara very consciously used this term to describe anyone working with children regardless of the qualifications they may have held. Similarly, the term 'school' is used although this sometimes describes settings where there are very young children.

The editor is aware of the debate surrounding the use of words such as 'special needs' and 'mainstreaming', but has retained them as they are included in the original and were considered appropriate at the time it was written.

Introduction

I recall Elizabeth Prescott's words when describing research in day care centres: 'In the beginning we did not know how to see very much when we visited centres.' I have felt over a series of observations that preconceptions about a situation fade as we see more clearly what is actually occurring. Second, Prescott suggests that the activities as named by the teacher do not necessarily reflect those as experienced by the child. This was outstandingly clear in my observations in a centre where the morning is in 30-minute divisions, alternating indoors and outdoors. The indoor 'class times' could certainly be titled in a variety of ways.

The crux of my interest is the feeling that a quality early childhood teacher can do a great deal for children who are mainstreamed. Teachers should feel competent about handling children with special needs and feel confident that a quality program can give such children many opportunities for development. A concern of mine is that the more specialist consultants there are on hand to help the teacher, the more dependent we become on them, and the more inclined we are to label children so that we can get that specialist help.

In my experience, there were many difficulties associated with the specialist consultants visiting centres, seeing children briefly, giving advice on programming, and then leaving until the next visit several months later. No one was happy. The consultants felt that the teachers were not giving enough individual attention to each child (defined as withdrawing the child from the group and giving him or her special activities designed to promote particular skills and development). The teachers expected that the consultant would visit and, as if by magic, the child's problems would be cured. Each was expecting the impossible of the other.

I am not sure this system is the best we can do at the moment and I am not suggesting we scuttle it. What I am suggesting is that teachers in centres where special-needs children are mainstreamed can promote their development more effectively through the medium of play and by following the children's lead. My observations over the last months have confirmed that if early childhood teachers follow the cues that mainstreamed special-needs children give us, we will be able to take them on the next steps in their development.

Consider this point: children—all children, and particularly special-needs children—need adults who interact with them, and 'it is important that we view children as completely competent for the stage they are currently in' (M. Gerber, in a Pacific Oaks College class). This statement helped me make a shift in my way of looking at children with special needs. I think it could also help teachers facilitate these children's progress as an 'add-on' to their current competence rather than as a compensation for the deficits.

Centres at which I observed this included:

1. A special school which catered to children with severe disabilities who, it had been agreed, could not be mainstreamed.

2. A school where approximately 50 per cent of the children had a range of disabilities—some very severe, some mild and some almost unnoticeable.

School One: an example of a school for children with severe disabilities

The facilities and services of the school were excellent. The ratio of staff to children was normally 1:4, but on the day I visited there were secondary students on community service for a 1:1 ratio. I visited the preschool class, with an age range of four–eight years. I noticed:

- a lack of interaction with some children and disproportionate attention given to others;
- an emphasis on routines and the preparation for carrying out these routines. Going to the toilet seemed to be given high priority, particularly for two of the children;
- that the activities offered in support of goals did not seem particularly appropriate for these children;
- that children were taken off one at a time for speech sessions.

A child confined to a wheelchair worked on a shape board, one-to-one with a teacher. The child experienced some success. I was not able to tell whether he could do the correct placing of pieces in his head. The control of movement was difficult for him, so it was hard to tell if the results were deliberate or accidental. He was more successful with a mail box, but I felt that the goal (to drop the piece into the box, thus losing it) may not have been the goal of the child, who seemed not to want to let it go. However, that may have been his physical lack of control.

Elsewhere, a tiny, fragile-looking child was being walked about, controlled completely by an adult. I wondered about the value of such an activity for the child. Could she take no control of whether she wanted to walk or not? In a group time, when each adult sat with a child in a circle and threw or rolled a ball across the circle, this child again had no control. It may be that the movement was very important for her, but it looked so painful and pointless that I questioned it.

Again, a boy who was blind, perhaps five or six years old, was showing interest in singing. A visitor suggested that he might like to have the nearby radio on, but the teacher said she preferred not. So he went on singing and rocking, in a self-stimulating way. I thought it was an instance when an adult could have intervened successfully in his isolation—perhaps singing and listening with him, or dancing and clapping. With excess adults available, was an opportunity being missed? When it was time for the circle game with the ball, this child was compelled to join in. He protested furiously. The teacher said he could have just one turn and then go. He managed well and was able to pass the ball.

Greenspan talks of the importance of giving children some opportunities to have control over their lives (Greenspan 1985). If the adult can let the child take charge some of the time, the child is likely to be more cooperative other times when the adult must take control.

Some of the children were severely physically disabled and in wheelchairs. Several were physically capable but intellectually delayed. On a one-day visit it is difficult to judge what is happening for the children. I hesitate to say that there was lack of interaction, but certainly some of the one-to-one activities seemed pointless, and other opportunities were missed. The IEPs (the Individual Educational Plan for each child) seemed taken directly from the educational system rather than from what children with particular disabilities might need. For example, is recognising squares and triangles essential for a child strapped from head to foot in a wheelchair? What are suitable goals? Who makes the decisions? Who would be able to contribute to goal-making? We seem so stuck in the 'school' groove, whereas what we need is a more imaginative and flexible approach.

School Two: an example of a school with a 50 per cent disability rate

There were three age groups: infant (2–18 months), toddler (18 months–3 years), and preschool. The children have 'home' groups but are free to mingle at appropriate times during the day. I observed Cindy, aged five, playing outside with her two-year-old twin brothers. Children without special needs are accepted, enrolments permitting.

A music session included ten children with three adults. It was joined by a toddler, who was welcomed by the teacher and set on an empty chair next to the teacher. After music time and an hour of outdoor play, the older children went in two groups to 'classes' while the younger children prepared for lunch. There were five children with a teacher in the group I observed. The activity involved placing pieces of yarn on an outline of a shape drawn on cardboard, with glue. The teacher prepared the glue shapes (triangle, square, rectangle and circle on each cardboard) while the children watched. She was adept in her control of the glue, and I felt that the children were watching with a similar awe to my own.

The children placed the yarn around the shapes with varying degrees of success. The activity required fine motor control, and in several cases the teacher finished the work for the child. When this task was done, they had to decorate the inside of the shapes with coloured rice. The teacher put glue in the middle of each shape and instructed the children to smooth it over the area. One child, Justin, objected, but the teacher explained that she had made the decision and he didn't have a choice. He complied. Some of the children were called away in preparation for lunch. The teacher finished the cards for those who left and did one for a child who was absent. Two boys were quizzed on the names of the shapes and asked to point some of them out in the room. A child called Charlie responded fairly confidently, whereas Justin had an embarrassed or quizzical grin and guessed at answers, apparently at random. He was not told he was wrong, but clearly he was aware that he didn't know! The 'class' ended, and the teacher explained to me that some of the children were doing well at learning the shapes and some were 'not so good yet.' She added that most of them were not yet four.

The outdoor time was very free, with the age groups mixed. The children spread over the whole area and pottered about at their own pace. They merged in and out of group and solitary play. I observed several instances of pretend play.

Cindy and Lindsey were packing pretend lunch boxes, using a large hollow building block and small plastic shapes. Cindy called one round shape a bagel; the squares, bread; and the triangle, cheese; and she saved one round shape for a doughnut. She made a sandwich and pretended to eat it. Lindsey followed Cindy's play with interest and collected a similar box and contents for herself.

Charlie and Peter were using assorted plastic items as guns. They were playing together, Charlie leading and Peter following. The game seemed to involve running a bit, finding someone to shoot at, then running off again. No one who was shot at responded, and the boys did not seem to need a response. They kept each other going. At one point Charlie pushed Peter away, saying, 'don't follow me', but the game went on in the same fashion.

A boy on a walking frame, Juan, was sitting in the dirt with a model house. Carefully, he picked up handfuls of dirt, letting it pour into the chimney and run down. Then he poured sand down the staircase.

The purpose of my first visit was to get a feeling for the structure of the day and to look for opportunities for self-directed play—or any kind of play. My first impressions were positive. Here was a school where the individual progress of each child was top priority. However, as I continued to visit I was gradually able to see more—including missed opportunities and misdirected efforts. I present these observations not to be critical or destructive, but to highlight the fact that we put enormous energy into attempts to guide children towards adult goals. If we could only be patient and take the leads the children give us, our energy would be so much better spent. I chose two target children to observe on repeated visits: Maria and Jorge.

Maria (aged four and a half)

Maria was born prematurely, at 31 weeks gestation. Her milestones are all delayed. She has visual impairment and echolalia. After one year in preschool, her echolalia is improving. She plays alone.

Observation one

Maria was walking about the yard. She had collected a shovel, a red dish, a yellow plate and a small yellow plastic bear. She had some difficulty protecting 'her things' from others. The teacher commented that she had never seen Maria defend her possessions.

Maria sat at the table next to the teacher and me and arranged her things. The yellow plate was placed toward the centre of the table, with the bear sitting in it. She took the red dish and scooped sand into it with the shovel, squatting on the ground next to us. Then she sat at the table and said, 'bear food'. There followed a pretend game of feeding the bear:

Maria: Bear food, bear food, too hot. (she blew gently into the sand in the red dish)

Teacher: How can you cool it, Maria?

Maria: Ice cubes in it. We have to cool it. (another child snatched away the red dish, but Maria followed up, saying, 'I have one,' and pulling the red dish back. The teacher said, 'Yes, but that's yours and you are busy with it.' This comment seemed to help Maria stand her ground with the offending boy. She got the dish back and returned to the table, where she sat to get on with her play. She fed the bear by using the red shovel with sand from the red dish)

Maria: Eat bear, eat bear. He throw up! (she looked at the adults with a surprised expression. We responded with like surprise. Her smile verged on the mischievous.)

Maria: He throw up! (Maria picked up the bear and smacked him. She looked closely at him. The teacher responded with, 'Oh, poor bear,' and Maria immediately tucked the bear under her chin and hugged him, then kissed him. Then she sat him back in the yellow plate and began the feeding again)

Maria: Eat bear, good boy, good food. Pick up that spoon. Eat bear. Sit, sit there! (with some aggression in voice) Bear, eat, bear. Look at me, open your eyes.

This conversation and comments went on for approximately 20 minutes after lunch, with an interruption for a trip to the toilet, after which it resumed.

On a previous visit I had seen Maria alone with a little shovel in the sand, just moving sand around and making no connections with adults or children. When adults directed her, she gave the appearance of not having heard. Sometimes she repeated the command and then carried it out. She was very obedient.

This time, however, the teacher was amazed by Maria's behaviour. She explained that Maria rarely positioned herself near anyone, that she had never before heard Maria talk except to echo someone, and that it was clear that Maria was playing out her own lunch-time experiences, even to the point where she often gagged on food when 'hurried'. Further, she was protecting her possessions, whereas she usually gave way.

Observation two

At the end of the song session two children were asked to help put away the children's chairs. Maria stood up, turned and picked up her chair by the seat, and was moving to put it away when Kevin grabbed it from the back. They struggled, pulling it from each other. Maria put up a good fight, saying firmly, 'mine, mine'. Suddenly an adult noticed and in a loud voice said, 'Maria!', her intonation implying that Maria was wrong. Maria immediately gave way, and Kevin put the chair by the table.

I did not know if Kevin was a chosen helper. But Maria looked close to tears as she walked towards the door, and as she went past me I stopped her and talked about what I had seen. After all, it was her chair!

Outdoors, Jorge was settled with a red plastic shovel and bucket, his walking frame next to him. He and an adult were putting sand into the bucket. Maria approached with another shovel. Moving quietly and slowly, she took the red bucket by the handle. Jorge watched with a serious expression. Maria moved around the walking frame and Jorge and sat down on the other side of him, placing the bucket between her legs in a position that allowed Jorge to reach it as well. Together they gradually filled the bucket with sand. Maria talked a little in her usual quiet voice. Jorge said nothing. When the bucket was nearly full of sand, Maria stood up and took it to the table under the tree. She emptied the sand onto the table and played with it for a while. She took the bucket back to Jorge, who had, in the meanwhile, been moved by an adult onto a little horse with wheels.

Observing the lunch-time activities, I understood the source of Maria's previous 'eat, bear' play. The children bring their own lunch and sit in small groups to eat while the adults stand over them. Maria was eating spaghetti from a bowl with a spoon and appeared quite interested in the food. 'Good girl, Maria,' said a staff member. Adults' comments to individual children, made in loud voices for everyone to hear, included 'eat', 'one more mouthful', and 'that's good'. The lunch process felt hurried; I wondered what they were hurrying for!

Observation three

During the song group Maria showed her feelings through body language and facial expressions. She smiled and laughed at words in the song 'My baby' about changing a baby's diaper, but by the time the song was over, Maria had just organised the doll up the right way to be changed. I felt that the pace was too speedy for her; she missed out because she needed more time. Some of the children were better at jumping middle bits, but Maria was thorough. I saw her almost visibly thinking through the activities.

Outdoors, Maria was moving about. She ran to have a couple of swings, then to the wheeled horse for a brief ride, and finally to the whirligig, where she shouted at Christopher, 'I want to get on! I want to sit on!' Christopher let her on, then looking closely at her glasses and eyes, kept saying 'one eye' over and over. She sat quietly, letting him inspect her. (I saw her as appreciating any contact and cooperating in order to preserve it.) The teacher called across the yard to Christopher, 'Stop touching Maria's glasses!' Christopher stood back, but he continued to talk to Maria, who responded.

Maria came to sit at the table next to me, with a doll and food and shovels. Feeding play similar to that I had observed previously went on, but this time she had ice cream, a very positive experience:

Maria: Yum, yum! (she hit the cone and licked the ice cream. Another girl attempted to take her doll and Maria pulled away, shouting) No, my baby!

Teacher: No, Maria is happy and wants to play with the doll.

Maria (to observer): I am happy! (she danced about, jigging on one leg and then the other. Then she sat on the bench next to the observer. Annie is on a horse near by)

Maria: Here, Annie, ice cream. (Maria threw the 'ice cream' to Annie. It fell short, but she jumped up, picked it up and handed it to Annie, who accepted it. Annie continued to rock on the horse, holding the ice cream)

When Maria returned to the seat, she said in passing to an observer, 'I make a little chocolate.' Maria often talks in passing, looking away so that it is difficult to tell who she is addressing. However, she seems very appreciative of a response and will go back to continue an interchange, though still not making eye contact. (I don't know how severe her visual impairment is.)

Another time, Maria was on the swing, a teacher encouraging her to pump herself. She seemed to get the rhythm. She also figured out a way to start the swing with a big arc, lying in it before pulling to a sitting position.

Maria seemed to be making real breakthroughs during the four weeks of my observations. The swing was one example—such a great sensation, to be feeling its rhythm! She seemed thoughtful towards others, as when she gave Annie the 'ice cream'. And one morning, working on a puzzle, she demanded adult attention: 'Look at me!' She seemed more assertive each week, and her assertiveness showed at appropriate times. Her comment, 'I'm happy,' was not an echo but a strong confirmation. When I heard her repeat words, her timing convinced me that she was not echoing but repeating with real purpose, to sort out meanings. (I had the feeling that Maria experienced my presence and interest as supporting her efforts, but I had no way of ascertaining this.)

Observation four

In the morning before circle time, Maria sat on the swing, pumping herself up high with excellent actions, obviously exhilarated. She mastered pumping in a week. She swung continuously for 15 minutes until called indoors.

Observing circle time, I noted again how fast-paced it always was. Most of the children were a couple of lines behind the action. Some seemed able to skip bits and catch up; others looked bewildered most of the time, though not unhappy. This particular day, Maria was able to keep up. She focused her attention on the teacher, her clapping was in time with the singing and music, and she marched in time with the recorded rhythm. She hung on to the main thread that interested her and filtered out all the extraneous happenings (other children being reprimanded, children talking, visitors and interruptions from other adults). It seemed to me the focus was continually changing—how would a child know what to follow?

Following circle time, Maria was told, 'you can go outside now'. She ran on tiptoes straight to the same swing (the one with longer ropes). She took the ropes in each hand, backed up to the extended swing, and jumped so her bottom landed on the seat and the swing moved in an arc. She swung up with good rhythm, legs tucked under on the back swing, arms extending her body back on the forward swing. She made the change from extension to flexion at just the right moment, and her expression reflected her success. 'I'm going to the tree!' she said.

I watched Maria swing for half an hour. She kept up the same rate, a half-smile on her face, her eyes fixed on a target which appeared to be the leaves of the tree. They were just outside the arc of the swing and at about the same height as the swing frame. Maria then ran on her toes from the swing to the bike path, where she climbed on a tricycle. She looked at the observer and said, 'I'm going to the market.' The observer nodded.

Maria banged into Cindy, also on a tricycle. Cindy said: 'Hey! Can't you find a parking spot? I can't too!' They untangled themselves, both pushing back with legs on the ground. Maria rode on to the end of the cement, dismounted, and ran to the swing close by (this time the one with shorter ropes). She was swinging again!

After lunch, Maria ran straight to the swing with the shorter ropes, talking loudly as she approached. Her running and noise caused Annie to get off the swing. She backed into the swing, jumped up, and in three swings was at top speed. Her expression changed from serious to a half-smile. On the forward swing she let her head drop back, moving her hair—one, two, three times. Her movement was synchronised with Kendra's on the next swing, but there was no apparent recognition of one by the other. Maria, on the forward movement, said 'da daaa!' repeatedly.

Maria stopped the swing by dragging her feet in the dirt. She moved away, then back. Kendra stopped too and lay across the swing seat with her hands and feet in the dirt. Maria knelt on the seat, holding the ropes, then hopped off. Then she put a foot on the seat and stood up on the swing. She jiggled it, then got off. She lay across the swing as Kendra was doing, running her feet and moving her body to swing forward several times.

Kendra left and Kenny replaced her. Maria looked towards Kenny. She stood up, sat on the swing and began to pump, and for several minutes had another satisfying swing. Kenny moved away. Maria dragged her feet to stop her swing, went to the other swing, and touched the seat: 'Kenny! Kenny!' She went back to her swing and held one rope while looking around: 'Kenny, Kenny, where are you?' She moved towards some children on tricycles making a noise. (I was reminded of her visual difficulties as I watched her searching.)

Then Maria saw Kenny, who was involved with two other children on a rocking boat. She seemed satisfied with having found him. She looked at him and touched him but didn't get his attention and didn't seem to need to. She returned to the swing and said loudly: 'Get off my swing!' The girl who was on it did, and Maria had another extended swing.

What a swinging morning she had had! Maria had gained confidence; she was moving about more, and faster. She had found ways of achieving and connecting with very little adult assistance.

Jorge (aged three and a half)

Jorge is delayed because of cerebral palsy. He's quadriplegic, and hyper-
tonic on the right side. He moves about in a walking frame and has
no expressive language.

Observation one

When Maria carefully picked up his bucket, Jorge watched intently.
When she returned it to where he could reach it, he slowly put in
one or two shovelfuls, but he took more time watching Maria. She
talked a little, not expecting a response. (I don't think Jorge has speech,
but it's just a matter of time judging by the look on his face.)

Maria took the bucket away. Jorge was lifted onto a little horse
with four wheels on which he appeared to sit quite comfortably. He
touched and looked at the reins and the tail. He pushed the horse
back and forth a little—not easy to do on a sandy surface! Maria
returned the bucket and shovel to Jorge. From astride the horse he
used the shovel to put a little sand in the bucket. He put the shovel
down, picked up the bucket, emptied the sand out, moved the bucket
upside down and looked inside it.

Jorge was lifted off the horse. He crawled to his frame and took
running steps with it towards the play room. Negotiating doormats,
small steps and corners, he got indoors, where he dropped to the floor
and crawled on all fours to the small room for teacher-directed
activities.

Outdoors again, Jorge sat on a tricycle, walking it along quite well,
steering with apparent ease and making a regular pace with alternating legs. (His practice with his frame probably made the tricycle a
simple task.) He put his feet on the pedals and seemed to know he
should push, but because of the very slight slope of the cement path
he did not have sufficient strength to keep it moving. (I think he will
be a successful rider in about a week!)

Observation two

Jorge now had leg braces and did not use his frame so much. Outside,
he sat in the sand with a shovel and placed dirt on the seat of a rocker,
spreading it thinly with precision and apparent care. As he worked, he
also looked around at all the other things going on.

During a small group painting activity, Jorge seemed eager to participate. Each child had a pot of thickish blue paint and a brush. Jorge took his brush at first opportunity and painted blue onto his paper.

Observation three

Jorge sat on the steps of the playhouse, watching children riding tricycles. The teacher carried a tricycle to him. He got up and began to move, not to the tricycle but around the side of the house, along the fence to the water fountain. The teacher moved Jorge into position so he could reach the water spout, then pressed the button. He moved his head so the water squirted into his mouth. He smiled broadly, pleased with the sensation and the result.

The teacher then held his arm to help him walk to a tricycle in the middle of the yard. 'Do you want to ride the bike?' she asked. Jorge shook his head. 'No,' he said quite clearly. (This is the first time I heard him speak.) Shaking his head, he pointed towards his walking frame. They walked to it, he took both handles and stood watching the other children. Then he dropped slowly to his knees and sat. He picked up a plastic doughnut shape from the ground and manipulated it onto his fingers, first in one hand and then the other. He tried fitting it onto the handle of the walking frame. For about ten minutes he manipulated the doughnut and gazed around at other children at play.

Karen approached Jorge. She patted his head, leaned over and looked into his face, and spoke to him. He slowly looked up and smiled—as she walked off with another child who was talking to her. Karen did not wait long enough for a response: Jorge's smile occurred as she walked away. This is also what I observed happening in Jorge's interactions with adults. I saw few opportunities for Jorge to prove his competence except at lunch time, where he manages his food, feeds himself, eats well and with enthusiasm, and seems very aware of what is going on around him. There is a chance to pace oneself at lunch time, in his class.

At class time the first activity was a memory game in which cards which lay face-down had to be turned over and matched. Jorge, in place at the end of the seat, was left out. Next, play dough was distributed. Jorge broke a ball of dough into pieces. He rolled a good, even-sized snake. The teacher intervened and rolled some of the dough out flat, then left. Jorge lifted the dough from the table and tore small pieces from it—good exercise for his fingers, which he managed well. There was some inaudible 'chat' with the boy next to him. This experience, though brief, seemed positive; Jorge appeared relaxed and sometimes smiling. After the adult removed the dough, Jorge rested his hands and his chin on the edge of the table. He yawned several times.

Next the teacher gave each child a sheet of paper and scissors—but there were no scissors for Jorge. The teacher muttered to herself, 'Oh, Jorge, there aren't any more.' Jorge looked around the table and at the child next to him. He didn't look at the teacher. No feelings were visible on his face. Then, one of the adults managing lunch picked him up from behind and without comment carried him into the bathroom and on to lunch.

After lunch, Jorge was again carried to the bathroom. About 15 minutes later I wondered where he was, and asked another adult to retrieve him from the toilet. He seemed unruffled by his long wait. He was sent outside on his walking frame.

Outside, Jorge was given a bucket and spade by an adult. As she handed it to him, she asked if he wanted it—then moved away without giving him time to answer. He began flicking the dirt with the spade, sending it quite a distance. Then he tried to enter the playhouse with the walking frame—a long process of manipulation of the walking frame and his body. Once inside, he turned and with great difficulty began trying to get the frame out. He got down and crawled under the frame, down the step to ground level, then turned and attempted to pull the frame after him. It was stuck in the doorway. Cindy, aged five, went to help. As she moved to lift the frame through the door, Jorge stood and moved to one side to make room for her. She manoeuvred the frame adeptly and then ran off. Jorge took the frame and walked across the concrete to the room.

Observation four

A passing teacher removed Jorge's sweater. As it came off, Jorge found that he was wearing a toy watch. He appeared surprised and pleased. He touched it, with some difficulty getting his hand to his wrist. No one commented on his watch. At circle time Jorge flicked his hand at Dominique. She pulled away from him, and he smiled at her response. She leaned back towards him a few minutes later. Jorge went back to examining his watch. He seemed to be enjoying the effort of manipulating it with his fingers.

During singing time Jorge attempted some of the actions suggested by the teacher. One of the songs called for everyone to 'move over'. Jorge was assisted, as were most of the other children, to move onto the next chair. During the story, Jorge looked at Ian. He leaned over and touched Ian on the arm. Ian was absorbed in the story, sucking his thumb, and did not respond to Jorge.

During outside time—approximately 30 minutes—Jorge walked out on his frame and sat by it for the entire time, watching the other children. When it was time to go in, Jorge got himself inside, but then the teacher sent everyone outside again for some reason unknown to me. As soon as they were out, she called them in again. This is all right for children who can run in and out, but it's tough for Jorge, for whom mobility is a problem. He was always last. At class time, when he was actively participating in activities (he definitely said 'apple'), he was carried off to lunch while the other children were still busy. Because of his slow mobility he missed out on some activities—though never on routines.

With little expressive language, Jorge elicited very little verbal response from adults. They lifted him about and left him isolated for long periods. Although he appeared to be on the brink of speaking, he was not given many opportunities to try. Often an adult would ask him a question and, before Jorge had time to respond, also answer it. When other children made contact with him, they appeared to expect no response.

Jorge seemed to be content to sit and play in the sand and to watch others at play. He was not at all demanding, and mostly adults ignored him. Missing out on things seemed to be a recurrent theme for him. I find myself hoping that as he develops some speech, he will learn to make demands as well.

Discussion

While speaking of children with special needs in general, as I am doing here, it is important to keep in mind the wide variety of disabilities, each with its own particular features and needs.

Many children with special needs lack spontaneity. They are more dependent on stimulus from an adult, such as modelling the use of a material. There seems to be a risk attached to this difficulty. The adults realise that the child is dependent on external stimulus, and with this realisation comes a parallel understanding that the child may not make a response to the stimulus, or that if a response is made its 'message'

is not of great value. Time and time again I saw an adult provide a stimulus and the child respond, but because the response occurred after a time lapse, the adult in the interim had left the scene and missed the response. Often such responses would have provided positive reinforcement for teachers, had they been aware of it.

Children with special needs frequently get stuck at the sensory-motor stage; that is, the practice stage. They are not provided with props that would encourage them to proceed to the symbolic stage. Such props, if available and accessible, provide a means for adults to model pretend behaviours. This is important, as often children with special needs are unable to make the transformations necessary for the development of symbolic play.

Children with special needs may have difficulty in communicating, which in turn affects their ability to connect with other children in social interchange. Frances Hawkins' (1974) description of the play of children who are hearing-impaired highlights the need for adults to be in tune with children's non-verbal cues. Where children are mainstreamed it is just as important that adults assist other children in developing sensitivity to these cues. I have seen children make approaches but not succeed, and I believe an adult could have assisted in these attempts.

Not only do children with special needs have limitations because of their disabilities, they are also subjected to tests, checks, therapy and interference of various sorts. With all these compulsory activities they simply have less time for fun. It is important for teachers to be aware of this and to make time for fun in the program. Because Jorge, for instance, had to fit into the schedule of the centre's routines, he continually missed out on activities that could have benefited him and given him pleasure.

With all young children our aim is to encourage independence. Independence is even more important for children with disabilities, yet some environments inhibit independence by requiring children to request assistance. If materials and equipment are not easily available, adults control their use by controlling the storage. Self-help is not expected or promoted.

Do teachers need to be needed? They could set up the environment to free themselves for involvement in sustained interactions with children, instead of being constantly in demand to provide for the children, thus interrupting their social interactions. The physical organisation of the centre can support, or inhibit, the goal of encouraging independence on the part of the children. The way in which areas are set up can also promote social contact between children. For example, a rocker requires two children to make it work effectively; a table set for two enables two children to get to know each other as they play. The types of materials and their arrangement are critical to the amount of spontaneous play elicited (Fallen & Umansky 1985).

The organisation of the environment needs to work both for children with special needs and for their teacher. Limited conditions seriously affect children's play development and, in turn, decrease the number and quality of opportunities for learning, practising and refining new skills. Fewer opportunities for fun add to the burden created by the disability. For these reasons, those who work with children with disabilities and their families must be sensitive to children's limitations regarding play, knowledgeable about the sequence of play skill development, and inventive in the creation of play activities and adaptation of materials according to individual needs (Fallen & Umansky 1985).

I am convinced that a good early childhood teacher with a strong background in child development has much to offer children with disabilities. If those children are candidates for mainstreaming, they are also candidates for success in our care. However, some rather alarming research (Stipek & Sanborn 1985), looking at teachers' interaction with disabled and non-disabled children in preschool settings revealed that, in relation to the disabled children, teachers were:

- more likely to offer information and directives;
- more likely to interrupt activities;
- less likely to respond to requests for assistance;
- more aware of misbehaviour and more disapproving;
- more generous with praise.

I find this a discomforting list of tendencies. Prescott et al. (1975) describe thriving children as those who are able to make adults feel competent in the setting. In contrast, non-thrivers often make adults feel inadequate. Does a child with a disability somehow make the teacher feel disabled?

Research in Great Britain found that preschool teachers felt totally unprepared to work with children with special needs (Clark 1987). The same research found that mainstreamed children were isolated with little interaction with other children and, in some instances, adults. Yet adults provide the crucial link between the child with special needs and the preschool setting. They are the link between the child with special needs and the other children. They build the children's understanding of themselves and the growth of their self-esteem.

Much of the material that teachers are choosing to use with young children with special needs is 'watered down' school work, materials and activities unsuitable for preschoolers. Much of the 'teaching' that I observed appeared to involve testing children to find out what they knew, and giving information directed towards rote-learning not suited to young children. Children with special needs get plenty of testing in other arenas. Let's free them and us by replacing this type of activity with play time while they are in centres!

I was also concerned by the degree to which the day's schedule revolved around an adult time-frame. There seemed to be excessive pressure to keep to schedule. As a result, routines rated very high on the priority list at the expense of play time. I am not denying the importance of routines, but sometimes they seem to reflect adults' need to be seen by others as working. When all the children are settled, content and busy, adults who feel they have nothing to do seem inclined to fill in with a bathroom routine!

I found an example in one of the children I watched, an 18 month-old. Each day he went to sleep towards the end of lunch. The staff woke him, washed him clean, and sent him outside to play. Once outside, he perked up, but after 15 minutes, it was nap time. The adult's schedule cut across the child's natural rhythm; it would have made sense to me to take him straight from lunch to nap. Nor do I understand the rush that routines create. Eating lunch was often hurried, but lunch is such an opportunity for learning, why does it need to be rushed? Adults need to look at ways of adjusting to the children's time-frame, rather than imposing their own.

Conclusion

Are there means of making changes to better meet the needs of children who are mainstreamed and the adults who work with them? I believe that we should begin with Magda Gerber's suggestion cited earlier that we view children as competent for the stage they are in. If we do so, we will see our task as adding to children's competence and giving them more control, rather than making up for their deficiencies. If a child is mainstreamed, we need clear information about the purpose of mainstreaming. But we need to assume that mainstreaming serves the purpose of contact with other children, and it is up to us to ensure that children make those connections. We should be alert to the possibility of children's isolation that can occur.

Children with special needs require adults to form a relationship with them and offer intellectual companionship. It is not always easy to gauge their intellectual ability, but we should assume the need for content in our relationship with them and therefore offer shared experiences. The provision of materials and organisation of the space should be planned to work for both children and adults. Teachers need to use their creativity and inventiveness to extract every bit of value from the setting.

The adults' energy which is currently being channelled into 'teaching' and routines might be switched to learning through observing and participating in children's play. A change in the balance of the schedule might give children more time to progress at their own pace. 'Hurrying' is not helpful to any preschooler, least of all those who have a disability (Elkind 1981).

Books and an early interest in literacy should not be overlooked. The extraordinary story of *Cushla and Her Books* (Butler 1975) explains that while people who didn't know Cushla labelled her retarded, at home with her supportive family she was reading at three years and three months. Books can be another means of linking the special-needs child with the world.

A partnership with families and teachers is crucial so that home and school experiences are complementary and not contradictory. Families not only have a right to know what is happening to their children, but also an obligation.

Here is what we need to do:

- Develop a clear understanding of the purpose of placing a particular child in a mainstream setting.
- View children with special needs as competent for their present stage, and give them opportunities for control.
- Feel competent as a teacher and confident to provide for the child.
- Build into the program some time to observe the children and their interactions with environment, staff and peers.
- Be willing to look critically at what we think we do and what we actually do for children.
- Create a team commitment to help these children to grow.

If we make an effort to do these things, Dorothy Butler's words about Cushla could apply to all children with special needs: 'One could count on Cushla to try.' (Butler 1975, p. 95) These children are real triers!

For further thought and discussion

1. Have you considered play as a learning tool for children with disabilities? Given that this chapter suggests that it is, what do you think would be the starting point for developing a play-based curriculum for children with disabilities?
2. This chapter suggests that many teachers use 'watered-down' school work for children with disabilities. Can you think of some examples of this?
3. If you have children in your service, or the service where you are undertaking your field experience, take time to stand back and observe the interruptions to a child's self-directed experiences. Are the interruptions necessary?
4. Observe a child with disabilities during the lunch and morning and afternoon tea periods. What were the adults doing during these periods?
5. Observations are an important part of understanding children's development, including that of children with disabilities. Choose the observations written about one child in this chapter. What do they tell you about the development of this child?

References

Butler, D. 1975, *Cushla and her Books*, Horn Book, Boston.
Clark, M. 1987, 'Early education and children with special needs', *Psychology and Psychiatry*, vol. 28:3, pp. 417–25.
Elkind, D. 1981, *The Hurried Child*, Addison-Wesley, Boston.
Fallen, S. & Umansky, W. 1985, *Young Children with Special Needs*, Charles Merrill, Columbus.
Greenspan, S. 1985, *First Feelings*, Penguin, New York.
Hawkins, F. 1974, *The Logic of Action*, Pantheon, New York.
Prescott, E. 1987, 'Environment as organizer in day care settings', in Weinstein, C. and David, T. *Spaces for Children*, Plenum, New York.
Prescott, E. et al. 1975, *Who Thrives in Group Day Care?*, Pacific Oaks, Pasadena.
Stipek, D. and Sanborn, M. 1985, 'Teacher task-related interactions with handicapped and non-handicapped preschool children', *Merrill-Palmer Quarterly*, vol. 31:3, pp. 285–300.

Part 3

THE PLAY ENVIRONMENT, RESOURCES AND THE ADULT'S ROLE

Courtesy of Denise O'Hagan

Part 3

The Play Environment, Resources and the Adult's Role

Part 3 looks at resources and materials in children's play environments and the role of the adults in their play. It opens with Pauline Berry taking us, in Chapter 10, on a pleasant and enlightening walk through a child's playground. The playground is part of an early childhood centre which has been recently redeveloped, and during our walk we see the processes leading up to the redevelopment, while stopping to enjoy each play space and learning the reasons behind the changes and the benefits to the children. The emphasis is, throughout, on the creation of a more natural look, and Pauline uses anecdotes to demonstrate how the children use the various areas, and a plan and photos to help us visualise the garden.

Next we move on to Chapter 11, by Anne Stonehouse, to look at the role of play for infants and toddlers, and the role of the adults who work with them. Do babies play? The answer is clearly yes, as we already know from Elspeth Harley's introduction to babies and toddlers' play (Chapter 2). If we observe babies for even a few minutes, we can see that they play, as the following episode I saw clearly shows.

An adult was playing with a group of three babies on a mattress and cushions in a large playpen. One child, Damien, was relaxed and lying on his back with a bottle; another, Pauline was hanging over the playpen watching other children; and a third, David, was playing with a soft toy. The adult stepped out of the playpen for a moment and came back with a large plastic cube. She tipped the contents—dozens of brightly coloured, small wooden blocks—into the playpen. The noise immediately attracted Damien, who discarded his bottle, got unsteadily to his feet and waddled over to the adult. He plopped down and began scrabbling in the blocks with both hands.

At the same time, Pauline twisted her body around from the edge of the playpen to see what was happening. She walked across the mattress, bent over and picked up two blocks, one in each hand. She clapped them together and looked for a response, which she got immediately from the adult: 'Aren't you a clever one!'. Pauline shrieked with delight.

David crawled over nearer the box and his gaze went from one to the other. The adult was providing a commentary and Pauline continued to shriek with delight at each clap.

This play went on for approximately ten minutes—and the oldest child here was just one year old!

This sort of play, and the importance of learning through play for babies and toddlers, is discussed by Anne Stonehouse in detail. Anne's descriptions are supported by a conversation she has with Fiona and Darlene, two highly experienced practitioners working with babies and toddlers, who explain how they plan for play and what they see as the backdrop for play. Anne analyses the characteristics of play and looks at the role of adults in it, including family and early childhood staff—a theme which is picked up later as the role of play in relation to older children is examined (Chapter 13).

Is a multicultural and anti-bias approach important for babies and toddlers? Anne leads a discussion based around this approach and what it means for staff, which also forms the basis of the next two chapters. In fact, Anne's approach in Chapter 11 is complemented by the later chapters, which also look at anti-bias but focus instead on the play of three- to five-year-olds.

Next, Chapter 12 looks at play and persona dolls. An interview with the writers, Kerry Bosisto and Anne Howard, sets the scene for a description of their work with persona dolls. Many issues relating to the anti-bias approach are addressed by these two experienced preschool staff as they report on their research, 'Developing critical thinking skills in an anti-bias curriculum'. While the focus of their research is to raise racial awareness, from it they are able to draw other valuable lessons about bias. Kerry and Anne give us many ideas for implementing an anti-bias approach through the use of persona dolls. The involvement of families (the importance of which is highlighted in Chapter 11) is exceptional, as the samples of their writings in the persona dolls' diaries and their actions testify. Not only do children develop through the use of persona dolls, but so also do staff and many families.

The final chapter in the book, Chapter 13, examines the play of children from about three to five years old, and I stress that this age span is approximate. Chris, whom you met in the Introduction and will meet again in this chapter, would tell me that children as young as two years old can participate in this form of play. Experts, however, consider that it usually starts at three years of age, but you may have children that engage in it earlier.

The role of the adult in providing resources for, and observing, children's socio-dramatic play is discussed. Like many chapters, this one is based on the belief that young children learn:

- through self-directed, and sometimes teacher-initiated, play;
- through first-hand experiences, and support experiences such as books;
- through opportunities and time to play out experiences in a way meaningful to them;
- when they build new knowledge, attitudes and skills on existing knowledge, attitudes and skills;
- when adults support and provide for the play, and when adults trust the children to direct their own learning.

All these points are discussed, anecdotes used to illustrate them and, as with the episode of baby play earlier, the importance of actual observations is highlighted. The adult's role as planner is also discussed.

The content of the program should emerge from observations, from play ideas contributed by both adults and children, and from experiences and action re-enacted by children and facilitated by adults. A format for a play-based program is also presented, which fits in with the way Fiona and Darlene, in Chapter 11, code each of their experiences, although their coding is more comprehensive and offers a greater involvement of the families—one of its most appealing aspects. If you have not read Chapter 11 yet, and are interested in programming matters, you may wish to turn to it.

The anti-bias theme that influences a number of chapters in this book is also dealt with in this final chapter as we look at supporting and providing resources for children's play.

Competency-based training is not new in Australia, but training and assessing to the National Child Care Competency Standards is a new approach that the field is required to take. Of particular relevance here is the Appendix at the end of this book, which matches the content of each chapter with the nationally endorsed Child Care Competencies. This Appendix will be useful for trainers, teachers and lecturers implementing training to these competencies—for whom the book will provide many readings and references on which they can draw— as well as proving of immense value to students.

Chapter 10

A walk around Lucy's garden: a playground design to foster children's play and enhance learning

Pauline Berry

Introduction

A playground in an early childhood setting needs to be a place in which children can explore, discover and problem solve, and in which adults are free to act out roles to help children make sense of their world and have fun with others. As Dattner states, it 'should be like a small-scale replica of the world, with as many as possible of the sensory experiences to be found in the world included in it' (Dattner 1969).

Several years ago in Adelaide, Lucy's preschool was part of a research project looking at children's use of fixed playground equipment. The findings identified structures that were rarely used, noted the inadequacies of others, and highlighted areas of the playground that were not fully utilised. As a result of the project, the centre's management decided to redevelop the playground so that the children would have a wide variety of experiences available in an environment that was interesting, challenging and absorbing.

Redeveloping a playground

The playground was analysed using the scheme designed by Kritchevsky and Prescott (1969) to determine whether there was enough to do per child, whether there were enough choices, and whether there was sufficient variety to provide for a range of interests. A plan that opened up the whole of the play area to the children was drawn up (see Figure 10.1). It was designed to encourage children to discover and explore a variety of areas by linking them in

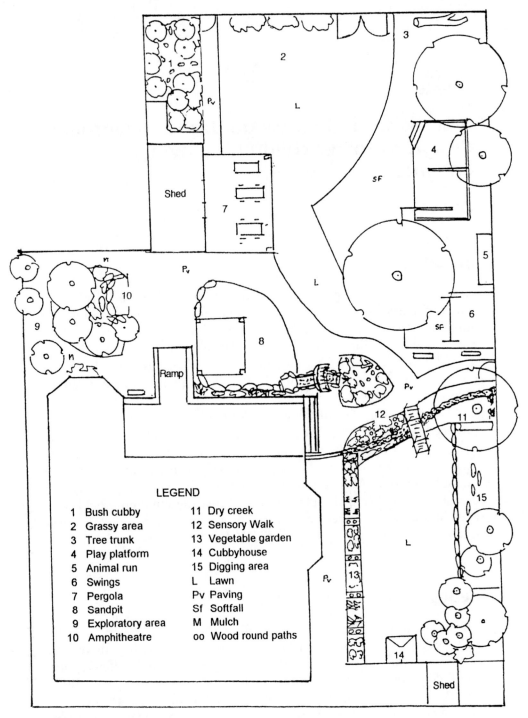

LEGEND

1	Bush cubby	11	Dry creek
2	Grassy area	12	Sensory Walk
3	Tree trunk	13	Vegetable garden
4	Play platform	14	Cubbyhouse
5	Animal run	15	Digging area
6	Swings	L	Lawn
7	Pergola	Pv	Paving
8	Sandpit	Sf	Softfall
9	Exploratory area	M	Mulch
10	Amphitheatre	oo	Wood round paths

Figure 10.1: Plan of a children's playground

different ways—with bridges, narrow inviting paths, secret or quiet places in which to play, and prominent parts.

Features of the new design

In the new design for the playground, every attempt was made to create as natural an environment as possible. The planners were aware that 'children don't experience some of our deepest childhood joys— those of field and stream, rocks and vacant lots; of privacy, secrecy and tiny things that crept across or poked out of the earth's surface' (Rivkin 1995, p. 2).

Bush cubby

As we enter the front gate, there is a secret bush cubby on our right with tree stump seats and soft bushy shrubs that would almost hide anyone playing in there. This area had been many things prior to the redevelopment, including a digging patch. Successful digging areas are messy and unattractive to adults; they shouldn't be the first thing seen by prospective enrollers visiting the centre. The bush cubby, in contrast, presents an attractive bushy garden to all entering the playground, as well as a wonderful cosy corner for quiet play.

Grass area

On the left side of the entrance is a cool grassy area with attractive flowering shrubs lining the fence. Here there is enough space for staff to set up an obstacle course, or for children to make constructions with outdoor building blocks or play ball games.

Thomas (four years, three months) and Ben (four years, four months) went into the nearby shed, carried out large wooden blocks and placed them on the lawn in the shade. When they had finished making their structure, they placed a steering wheel in the front of the blocks. The two boys climbed onto the structure. Ben sat in the front, and began turning the steering wheel and making motoring sounds.

'I'm going on a helicopter,' said Thomas.

'Dad's coming too,' said Ben, still driving the car.

'Are you going to watch me on the helicopters and aeroplanes?' asked Thomas.

'Yeah! Daddy's . . . I'll be there all the whiles. Do you want to come on with Daddy on the car?'

'No! I want to go on the helicopter,' said Thomas, as he climbed down off the car.

'I'll go,' said Ben. 'You can be the other driver.'

They both walked away.

'Hey!' shouted Thomas. 'We forgot to lock the door!'

The two boys turned around and walked over to the car.

'Lock,' said Ben.

'Lock,' said Thomas, and they both twisted their hands as if to turn the key.

Children often use their constructions as props or sites for their dramatic play. Sometimes the structure is built for a specific purpose; at other times the dramatic play evolves as a result of the construction. It is important, therefore, to allow children the opportunity to combine the two activities.

This grassy area used to have a metal climbing frame in the middle and, by the fence, an historic baker's cart which had become dangerous and out-of-bounds to the children. When the sun was at its height, the climbing frame heated up so much that children could burn their hands by just holding onto the bars. Our research found that 'of the

120 minutes of observation time, three children used the metal equipment for a total of eight minutes' (Berry 1993, p. 121). This was mainly to lean on while waiting for a turn on the jouncing board, and to store fire fighting equipment in fire station play.

The baker's cart reflected the custom, in this community, of giving special pieces of machinery to centres as they become obsolete in the workplace. Children love them and to adults they hold precious memories. However, pieces of machinery not specifically built for children can present many unseen hazards, particularly as they begin to disintegrate. For example, there can be entrapment features, sharp corners and hiding places for spiders—all unacceptable in a safety-conscious society. The baker's cart presented a real problem for staff and management when the time came for them to dispose of it, as it held a very special place in the hearts of previous students and parents.

In the far left-hand corner of the playground, previously little used, there is now an old tree trunk. Sometimes a saddle is placed on it and the children go 'galloping off into the distance'; another time it may be a quiet, watching place for a child unsure of how to join the play, or who needs to be alone. Next to the tree trunk is a tyre swing on the branch of a tree; the swing can double up as transport from the tree trunk 'house'.

A small, elevated cubbyhouse next to the tree, which was rarely used for dramatic play, was moved. It was lowered to ground level and placed on the edge of the lawn near the children's garden. Cubbyhouses above ground level are very hard to furnish as they require too much lifting for staff and make it impossible for children to take part in their furnishing.

Play platform

The cubbyhouse was replaced by a large, low, two-sectioned play platform, one section 300 mm high and the other 200 mm high, surrounded by softfall material. This structure is so flexible that it can be converted into whatever is needed. It has canvas sails that can be attached to protect children from the hot Australian sun or provide a roof when dramatic play calls for a home, office or hospital.

In the front of one section, movable climbing boards and ladders can be attached. Sometimes they are linked to an obstacle course to provide a variety of climbing experiences for the children; alternatively, a single ladder might provide another way onto the platform. The other platform has a ramp access for wheelchairs, pushers or other wheeled toys.

One platform can be used for construction toys, while the other has cutting and pasting activities on a table. One or both sections can be set up for dramatic play—whatever seems appropriate to the staff at the time. Neither of these platforms have any appeal without equipment, props or furniture, so their success depends largely on the skill of the staff in setting up, or allowing the children access to, props and equipment to develop their own play.

Emma (four years, eleven months) and Rebecca (four years, five months) were on the play platform. Emma pulled on a pair of rubber flippers and Rebecca did the same. 'Come on,' said Emma, as she dragged an old deflated blow-up mattress onto the softfall in front of the platform. 'Get in the boat!'

Emma began to imitate the sound of a motor as she sat on the front of the mattress, rocking to and fro. Rebecca struggled on to the mattress in her flippers. She had just managed to sit down with her flippers on and had begun to rock sideways when Emma said, 'I want to get out now, it's night-time.'

Rebecca lay down. 'You're not in the house yet!' said Emma. She pulled the rubber mattress out from under Rebecca and dragged it back up onto the platform. Both children had to lift their feet high so as not to trip over their flippers.

Rebecca stood on the platform in front of a sleeping bag. 'I'm going in there,' she said.

'Okay!' said Emma, picking up a towel and wiping herself down after being in the 'water'.

The two girls took off their flippers and climbed into the sleeping bags.

'Goodnight,' said Emma.

'Goodnight,' said Rebecca.

The play platform had been set up by staff following the interest shown by the children the day before. These two children had not been involved in the play previously, but the availability of the props prompted, and enriched, their play by allowing them to act out their roles. The availability of props or 'loose parts' (as Nicholson 1971, pp. 30–34, Frost 1992, p. 39, and Jones and Reynolds 1992, p. 23 term it) encouraged the children to be creative in their play.

Staff should be aware that the type of props provided can influence the type of play. As MacNaughton says: 'The gender politics of children's play may be expressed directly, or indirectly, by their choice of materials or activities.' (MacNaughton 1996, p. 5)

Many staff suggest that a play platform is not necessary as children will act out roles anywhere. However, a variety of locations with interesting props need to be available to provide sufficient areas for dramatic play. As preschoolers tend to play in groups of five or under, and preschool centres usually have about 30 children in a group, there need to be many cosy areas where children's play—dramatic play in particular—can develop.

Softfall material surrounds the play platform so that climbing boards and ladders can be set up. One of the cheapest and most effective softfall materials in Adelaide is a pine chip that will cushion children if they fall. The depth of this material depends on the height from which children may fall, and there are guidelines as to the recommended depth. Most centres opt for low platforms which reduce the risk—the lower the platform, the easier it is for children to take props into the area. Children continually use the softfall for 'food' in their dramatic play or for filling and emptying containers and, in some centres where the playground has little appeal, the softfall is used more than the equipment.

An animal run which is long and narrow is positioned under the shade of a large cedar tree next to the play platform. When the cedar tree is in fruit, it attracts colourful parrots to the area, which children can watch while playing. Chairs can be placed in the animal run so children can nurse and feed the rabbits or guineapigs. Often the animals are fed leaves from the children's own vegetable gardens.

Swings

The double swing was the only piece of equipment that was not repositioned in the redevelopment. It is already in a perfect position—close to the building so that shy children do not have to venture far to use it, nor do children have to run through the swing area to reach other activities. It is a good place in which to sit, swing and watch everything that is happening in the playground. Also, being a double swing, it allows friends to talk as they swing.

Children are very perceptive. They discovered that if they stand in the centre of the playground and watch other children at play, a staff member is likely to redirect them into some 'worthwhile' activity, whereas if they sit on a swing and watch, staff see this as a 'legitimate' activity and do not interfere. Children need a quiet watching place from which they can see all of the playground and check out the play before joining a group. The placement of swings is, therefore, very important.

Storage

The equipment shed is in a central position, allowing both staff and children to take equipment, props and blocks from the shed to nearby areas to use in their play. It is important to allow children access to props and building blocks so that they can add new elements to their play as the need arises.

A large pergola was built in front of the equipment shed. Tables and a woodwork bench are located in the shade to enable staff to provide table-top toys and activities as required. Many children use this area to make props or maps for their treasure hunts, or write and draw about their discoveries outside.

Sand and water

In front of the building, the old vine-covered pergola stands over a sandpit, to which a 'creek' leads from a nearby garden. The sandpit has

been upgraded to include a water-course, and enlarged to give the children plenty of space in which to dig, construct and solve problems. Children spend longer in a sandpit when there is water at their disposal—dry sand is limiting. A vandal-proof tap enables staff to regulate the flow of water into the creek. When access to water is by a hose, one child usually claims ownership of it and the others tend to miss out, whereas if the water enters the sandpit on a wide front, more children can use it at the same time. The 'creek' ends in a small pond in the sandpit that allows the water to enter the sand on several sides.

Trees

On the right-hand side of the sandpit is a stone amphitheatre and an exploratory area under trees. This corner was out-of-bounds, covered with weeds, rubbish bins and low scraggly plants. All the rubbish, weeds and plants were removed. A mulch path was placed under and around the trees, leading children into an ideal area for discovering snails, slaters and ladybirds. Children spend hours here, with and without staff, in small groups or by themselves, searching and observing the wonders of nature.

Chan (four years, eight months) gently picked a ladybird from a tree in the exploratory area. 'Oh!' he said softly, as it dropped to the ground. He picked the ladybird up again and, cupping his hands, inspected it as it sat in his hands; then watched it intently as it walked along his arm.

'Look! It's got its wings out now,' said the teacher.

The ladybird flew to the ground.

Tony (four years, three months) rolled over two stones edging the garden. 'Look, look,' he said pointing to two snails. 'Two comed out.' Sarah (four years, two months) stood watching.

'Have a look under the rocks,' said the teacher. 'If it's nice and damp under there you might find something.'

William (four years, six months) walked very slowly towards the teacher with a ladybird sitting on his thumb.

'See, he's on my thumb,' said William. Sarah grabbed his hand. 'Don't squash him!' William said. He held his hand up to Sarah's eye level, and they both watched the ladybird walking down his thumb.

The amphitheatre is often the scene of socio-dramatic play, usually sparked off by the placement of props in the area. Sometimes flippers, snorkels and masks will prompt 'underwater' play with the trees becoming seaweed and plants; picnic sets will encourage picnics or home play; and the paving in front will often be used for construction activities.

Bridge

A downpipe from the roof of the building takes stormwater from the building into an open drain, then out into the nearby street. Although narrow and seldom filled with water, the drain cut the playground in half and children seldom crossed over it to the grassy area beyond. During the redevelopment, a bridge recycled from the old cubby structure was placed over the drain, opening up the bottom end of the playground and giving children much more space.

There is a great desire in all of us, especially children, to cross a bridge to see what is on the other side, or to lean over its sides to gaze below, even if the bridge is just off the ground. When the bridge was placed over the drain, the intention was to have a dry creek bed that would allow the water to drain away in winter yet provide an

interesting place for play when it was dry—but the children had other ideas! They spent hours filling the watering cans and pouring water into the dry creek bed.

The whole area around the creek bed was planted with colourful flowering shrubs and perfumed plants, through which narrow paths led through to other interesting areas, creating walks that are truly sensory experiences. The narrow vegetable garden nearby allows children to water plants without having to walk over the garden. They can inspect the growth and pick vegetables, either for cooking or to feed the rabbits and guineapigs.

The main activity around the nearby cubbyhouse is water-painting. Cubbyhouses are of little interest to children without furniture or props inside, and this cubby is really too small to contain much activity. However, it has proved useful for the younger children whose play is either solitary or in twos, since there is just enough room for a tiny table and chair.

Digging

A large digging area has been created in the shade next to the side fence, replacing the old rectangular piece of hard soil in the corner with a light sandy loam, easy to dig, with large, interesting rocks in the middle to sit on or dig under, around and between. The digging area has a large tree trunk to sit on and easy access from the lawn. Children need a reason to dig—something to discover or unearth. This area is enticing to children who would not normally take part.

> One day, shortly after the summer holiday, a group of children were energetically digging a hole under a large stone.
> 'What are you doing?' a visitor asked them.
> 'We're digging to see if there is a wombat in the hole,' they replied. 'He could have come when we weren't here. Wombats live in holes, you know, and there could be one in here.'

Any wombat would probably have been cut in half by the vigorously wielded metal spades! However, the digging was serious business, and with input from the staff and children 'in the know', a great deal was learnt about wombats.

Conclusion

The redevelopment took place gradually over several years. Families and staff were involved, and professionals also, when necessary. With help from parents and staff, children established a 'plant bank', where they stored and watered cuttings and young plants in readiness for the final planting.

Working bees took place regularly, and parents gave up many a weekend to contribute. With their help, one parent who was a carpenter organised the construction of the very successful play platform. Every Monday, children would race into the centre to see what was new. When the structure was completed, the committee invited all the parents to the centre, where they enjoyed a celebratory sausage sizzle, accompanied by a jazz band playing on the platform.

As a result of this redevelopment of their playground, the nature of children's play has changed. Children are more absorbed as they make more exciting discoveries and master a greater variety of skills. Play is more sustained, with less aimless running around. Staff can interact with the children more easily, supporting their play and introducing resource materials and information to enrich their activities. There is shared pride in the centre, both in its appearance and in the program it provides.

For further thought and discussion

1. How many of your special childhood memories involve nature—empty paddocks, areas by the sea, creeks or other secret places to explore; pine cones, stones and shells to collect; trees to climb and cubbies to build? Are you providing the children in your life with these wonderful experiences? If so, how?
2. Children's play reflects what they know, how they think, what is important to them and the joy of discovery. How can you use this valuable information to further enrich their lives?
3. Many playgrounds are full of fixed equipment that cater for children's physical needs, but little else. Do you have sufficient variety of activities and experiences in the outdoors area to cater for your children's interests and needs?

References

Berry, P. 1993, 'Young children's use of fixed play equipment', *International Play Journal*, vol. 1, no. 2.
Dattner, R. 1969, *Design for Play*, MIT Press, Cambridge, MA.
Frost, J. 1992, *Play and Playscapes*, Delmar Publishers Inc., New York.
Jones, E. & Reynolds, G. 1992, *The Play's the Thing: Teacher's Roles in Children's Play*, Teachers College Press, New York.
Kritchevsky, S. & Prescott, E. 1969, *Planning Environments for Young Children: Physical Space*, National Association for the Education of Young Children, Washington DC.

MacNaughton, G. 1996, 'The gender factor', in *The Anti-Bias Approach in Early Childhood*, Creaser, B. & Dau, E. (eds), HarperEducational, Sydney.

Nicholson, S. 1971, 'How not to cheat children: the theory of loose parts', *Landscape Architecture*, vol. 62, pp. 30–34.

Rivkin, M. S. 1995, *The Great Outdoors*, National Association for the Education of Young Children, Washington DC.

Chapter 11

Play, a way of being for babies and toddlers

Anne Stonehouse

Introduction

Perspectives on play are abundant, resulting in, for example, highly structured, product-orientated, adult-directed activities being presented to children and sometimes mislabelled as play. It is not so much what is offered by adults to children in early childhood programs that makes it play or not-play, but rather how it is offered, and how much control and freedom children are given to construct the experience on their terms.

There is also confusion surrounding the role and even the definition of play in programs for the youngest children. Some practitioners working with babies and toddlers, suffering from low status and driven by a desire to be seen to be doing something educational, such as teaching, offer adult-organised and adult-directed activities with specified products or outcomes and call them 'learning activities'. Play is relegated to the category of time-filler. More commonly, at the other end of the spectrum, are those who believe that play is simply a matter of letting very young children 'do their own thing' with just any old bits and pieces; that they don't start doing any real learning until they are older. This view reinforces the mistaken notion that caring for under-three-year-olds is simpler and less intellectually demanding than working well with older children.

As is the case with many things, the truth lies somewhere in between these extreme views. Play with under-three-year-olds will indeed 'just happen', as with very young children, if they are healthy, safe and resourceful. However, if it is to be play at its best—play that maximises the opportunities for pleasure, success and learning—then adults have a major role to play, especially in group care. The adult is the architect of the environment for play, creating exciting places for under-three-year-olds to explore, experiment, and use their rapidly emerging skills. The adult is the gatekeeper, determining the access the child has to the environment. This perspective on the critical roles of the adult in babies' and toddlers' play is explained clearly in *Prime Times: A Handbook of Excellence in Infant and Toddler Care* by Greenman and Stonehouse.

A key focus in this handbook is the role of the caregiver as architect and engineer of the environment for learning: preparing a world at children's fingertips and maintaining environments for free and structured play. In earlier chapters our emphasis was on the caregiver as the adult who provides the security and stability that free young children to explore, develop their curiosity, and become involved in play. Infants or toddlers who are not sure that their needs will be met or who have to adjust continually to new caregivers, places and routines are less likely to get involved in active play and exploration. Another critical role of caregivers is that of supporting children's learning through interactions, interventions and language.

It is worth noting that the authors considered and rejected the term 'teacher' to describe the role of the adult working with under-three-year-olds, while acknowledging that it does confer 'educational legitimacy'. Why the concern over teaching? Because education is an inseparable component of good care and because learning happens all the time, including during routines and transition.

However, only rarely does teaching in the sense of instruction play a part in very young children's experience. Infants and toddlers acquire new skills and understanding about the world and themselves through play, exploration and living each new day. Good caregivers value and encourage play as a natural and integral part of their experience in day care. While caregivers need to be aware of children's emerging skills and probable next developmental steps, they do not need to program artificial or special activities to teach these skills (Greenman & Stonehouse 1997, p. 217–18). This sounds easy, but in fact it is more challenging than implementing a prescribed set of activities, because it requires responding at the right moments and in appropriate ways, rather than initiating. In other words, good caregiving necessitates handing over control to babies and toddlers.

It is a worthwhile exercise for practitioners with babies and toddlers to examine their own beliefs about the definition and role of play in day care programs for babies and toddlers, and periodically to reaffirm its importance and how best to provide for it. A conversation with Fiona Brodrick and Darlene Leach, two experienced and reflective practitioners who work at the Melbourne Lady Gowrie Child Centre with under-two-and-a-half-year-olds, yielded some interesting insights about the play and learning experiences of very young children. They live with the play of very young children and know it well. We attempted, in our conversation, to look at their play afresh and think about how it differs from that of older children. We reflected on why it is often under-appreciated and misunderstood, and tried to identify what is most important in providing for play for these young children, whatever the setting. Their ideas, with my own thoughts and comments added, are embodied in this chapter.

The essence of play for babies and toddlers

Fiona: Ask me to picture very young children at play, and I picture sensory experiences, something where they use their hands, their whole body, their whole being. Play means the child takes the lead, even when you are talking about a very young baby. The child has control.

Darlene: When I picture babies' and toddlers' play at its best, I think of total engagement and concentration—what might be called application to task, perseverance, unbridled curiosity, a combination of seriousness and sheer joy. I think you actually see that more with babies and toddlers than you do with three- to five-year-olds. Babies and toddlers immerse themselves in play, literally and figuratively. If they are fully engaged, they are playing with their whole being.

How play fits into a group program for babies and toddlers

Darlene: In day care for babies and toddlers, there is a lot of time spent in routine activities, but there can be a lot of play in routines. The more you let babies or toddlers be active partners and let them have some control over what is happening, the more the experience is like play. Nappy-changing and eating can incorporate elements of play.

Fiona: What we are really saying is that the higher the program quality, the less distinction there is between play and non-play. The better the overall experience for children, the more you see them engaged fully, taking the lead and being active participants—in other words, playing. With under-three-year-olds, you can't really say 'this is play, this isn't'. It's a continuum—it's more accurate to say 'this is more play, this is less play'.

The basis of the program for babies and toddlers

Fiona: At the Melbourne Lady Gowrie Child Centre provision for play is linked directly to the aims and objectives of the centre.

The section of the philosophy statement most relevant to play reads as follows:

We believe the role of the Children's Program is to meet the needs of the children while they are at the centre. We believe the children need to:

- feel safe, secure, respected, valued, cared for, happy, encouraged and reassured;
- know about themselves, others, the environment, routines and limits;
- acquire living skills, including social skills, language skills, physical skills and a respect for people and things.

The adult role in the program is to provide a nurturing, stimulating, responsive environment, and to interact with children in a way which makes learning possible. We believe children learn through play. Children's play takes a variety of forms, such as:

- modelling/imitating (adults and other children);
- observing;
- experiencing;
- discovering/exploring;
- contemplating.

Darlene: As we plan the experiences that form the basis for the curriculum, these forms of play, together with the children's developmental stages and their current interests, are taken into consideration. We provide a balance between child-initiated and adult-supported experiences in which children may use a range of equipment and materials, including improvised equipment and natural materials.

Differences in play for babies and toddlers

It is notable that there is a single statement for all age groups in the centre, including babies and toddlers. In some services there is the implicit assumption that issues pertaining to planning and organising experiences for the very youngest children are substantially different to those relevant to three- to five-year-olds. In some services this distinction is formalised by having a different statement of philosophy for the youngest age group. In spite of research, expert evidence, and protestations from wise practitioners to the contrary, the view that programming for under-three-year-olds is different is still held by some. For 'different', read simpler, easier, requiring less knowledge and understanding on the part of the adult.

Are there fundamental differences between the play of babies and toddlers and that of older children? Yes and no. There are obvious differences in developmental levels and abilities. The most profound difference is that the play of babies and toddlers merits more support and careful provision because it is fundamental, primal, and lays the foundations for skills, understanding and approaches to learning that will stay with the child. However, because it occurs so naturally, it is less well understood and is often less well catered for than the play of three- to five-year-olds.

In the play of older children, the adult's role relies to a greater extent on verbal contributions—suggestions, extensions and assistance with problem solving—and the contribution of equipment and materials; in other words, it is largely a facilitating role. Babies and toddlers are more likely to need an adult's physical presence and participation. Significant adults are significant playthings for babies!

Three characteristics of babies' and toddlers' play may help to explain why it is sometimes dismissed or trivialised:

1. If they feel safe and secure, a baby's or toddler's play is largely self-directed. Under-three-year-olds are resourceful human beings who are so open to the wonderful possibilities for pleasure, discovery, enjoyment and learning around them.
2. The younger the child, the more the play is likely to be investigatory, exploratory, process-orientated and seemingly without a plan.
3. The meaning and significance of babies' and toddlers' play may elude the casual observer. Its value is not obvious, and an adult

may take the view that 'if I don't see the value, then it's not valuable'.

In light of the characteristics of play outlined, what are the main roles of adults in babies' and toddlers' play? These three characteristics hold direct implications for the roles of people working with very young children.

First, a major responsibility for adults is to provide the conditions—the materials, space, time, security, assistance and support—for play. In other words, adults are the architects of the context for play. Second, it is essential, because of the subtlety, the 'non-obviousness' of the meaning of much of babies' and toddlers' play, for adults to have extensive understanding and wisdom about children's development in general as well as about the temperament, individual styles and interests of the individual children they work with. Third, this understanding of development must be translated into sensitive responsiveness to each child, responsiveness that affirms the child and the play. Fourth, the adult must be excited by young children, taking genuine delight in their struggles and accomplishments. The first three roles can be learnt, but the fourth—just as essential—adults cannot be trained in or taught. It has to be inherent, or it must be 'caught' through working alongside others who are excited and enthusiastic about young children and sensitive to their needs.

There is also a fifth implication, which is that adults who work with babies must be clear about what it is they are trying to achieve, and what their objectives are for the children. That is not meant in a strict educational sense, but in the broadest way. Staff must be aware of the values that lie behind their work with children, and the images they have of the children they work with. If these images are not of the child as strong and powerful, and if they do not embody respect for the child's choices about how and when to play, then the opportunities for the child to engage fully in opportunities for play will be diminished.

Development is not a race. In a good program, caregivers recognise the important skills that infants and toddlers are acquiring, delight in them when this occurs, and provide opportunities for children to use them when they are ready. They know that young children rarely need to be taught skills or pushed to perform; rather, they simply need opportunities, occasional help, and people who can share in their pleasure and achievements (Greenman & Stonehouse 1997, p. 27).

The role of parents in contributing to play in day care

Darlene: Strong links with families of children at any age are an important component of care for a variety of reasons, but are essential if day care staff are to support very young children's play. Parents' perspectives are necessary for staff to have an accurate and complete picture of a child's interests. Children's parents are indispensable as translators.

Fiona: Let me give you an example to illustrate that.

A two-year-old became fascinated with a bulldozer involved in some excavation in the block next to the centre. Each time he saw it he uttered a collection of sounds enthusiastically but completely unintelligibly. We noticed that he also used this utterance when pointing, again with great excitement, to cars. We attributed this to confusion about what is and is not a bulldozer, assumed a passion for bulldozers, and made plans to bring in some books about bulldozers and to make a toy one available for him in the sandpit. When we mentioned this fascination with bulldozers to his parents, they laughed, confirmed the sound that he had been making, and informed us that this was not a fascination with bulldozers, but with anything that had an exhaust, including the stove and the hairdryer at home! What he was actually saying was 'hot exhaust'!

Planning for children's play

Darlene: Appropriate provision for children's play brings together information and ideas from a number of sources, including:

- watching and listening to children;
- taking careful observations;
- insights and information from parents;
- the knowledge staff bring about what are appropriate experiences.

Fiona: Staff in the babies' and toddlers' room treat each of these sources seriously and try to ensure that what they provide reflects a balance of sources. In the written plans we prepare, a code for each experience that is planned indicates its source, and the staff use this system as one means of checking the quality of what they are offering. The code consists of the following:

CI: Child initiated—an experience or opportunity that is present in the environment for children to take up if they wish, based on knowledge of the children and what they enjoy doing, with the aim of supporting and extending their interest.

FO: Follows observation—an experience that is offered because of an observation that an adult has made about the child's developmental level.

PI: Parent initiated—an experience planned because of a suggestion or information from the parent about a particular interest of a child.

SI: Staff initiated—an experience offered as a result of an idea that a staff member has (from reading, a workshop, a suggestion from a colleague, or something that has worked well before).

The strongly held belief is that over time the program must reflect a balance of experiences from these sources, with the majority of them coming from our observations of children's development or interests.

Important ingredients for the 'backdrop' to play

Darlene: What provides the foundation for play? I think providing an environment that supports and encourages play, and Fiona would agree with me that stability and continuity are critical. It is important to make changes to engage the children's interests and match their increasing skills, but the environment should evolve gently, and changes should be gradual. Our hunch is that, as a rule, keen, knowledgeable caregivers, full of good ideas, may need to exercise restraint in making changes.

Fiona: Yes, babies and toddlers probably prefer fewer changes and surprises than we think. We believe that the key to making change successfully is tuning into the level of interest being displayed by the children and allowing that to be the criterion for judging when change is necessary.

Darlene: And we try to identify when the urge to make changes comes from our desire for novelty rather than children's boredom and find alternative ways to excite and enthuse ourselves. We also try to resist pressure from colleagues, parents or others to do something different, to offer activities mainly because they will impress other adults rather than the children!

Multiculturalism and anti-bias in play for under-three-year-olds

Fiona: We acknowledge that some people might say that there is little relevance, or that it is simply a matter of incorporating a variety of 'stuff' from other cultures in the environment and program: music, foods, pictures, home corner equipment, and so forth. There is a much more fundamental link, however; one that is not so obvious but much more important. It is through interactions with others that we acquire notions about:

- who we are;
- what we are good at;
- our value as a person;
- our power;
- the trustworthiness of other people;
- how gender affects what are considered appropriate behaviours and activities;
- whether or not other people are a threat; that is, whether or not they mostly bring pleasure or pain.

Darlene: Yes, in play and other ordinary interactions adults give children messages about all of these, and it is in infancy and toddlerhood that these messages begin to be absorbed.

Adults are children's most powerful models for learning, and through their play with them, as well as in their own words and behaviour, they teach children about:

- others' rights;
- responding to someone else's pain, sadness or fear;
- competition;
- cooperation;
- compromise;
- compassion;
- sharing and generosity;
- whether or not it is okay to look and act differently.

Babies and toddlers are learning fundamental messages about these things, which lie at the heart of tolerance of differences and appreciation for the needs, rights and feelings of others. It will, of course, take much longer than three years for a child to understand all of them, but they can be well on the way.

Fiona and Darlene referred again to the close links they have with each parent, and the continual efforts they make to use parents' knowledge about their children in order to program effectively for them. They encourage parents to contribute ideas and suggestions for experiences and ensure that these are incorporated into the programs. It is easier to embed a multicultural, anti-bias perspective naturally into every dimension of the program for babies and toddlers when there is cultural diversity among the families and staff. This is most often already the case in children's services throughout Australia. However, when it is not it is even more important to build in naturally occurring opportunities for children to experience differences comfortably and positively. This includes differences related to culture and ability. One powerful way to accomplish this is by ensuring that the composition of staff reflects a diversity of culture, language, age and gender.

Of course, it is likely that any group of children will consist of both boys and girls, which in itself affords opportunities to give children fundamental messages about equality of gender. In simple ways, caregivers can encourage both boys and girls to express their feelings, be gentle, caring, strong and powerful, and to be assertive—to be themselves in the richest, fullest sense possible. Books, stories and modelling by important adults are, of course, sources of important messages and 'teachings' about gender.

Conclusion

In summary, what are the keys to effective programming for this age group? According to the two experienced practitioners interviewed, the most important are:

- observing closely and really knowing all the children;
- being in tune with them—switching into what they are thinking and slowing down to a gentler pace (in spite of feeling at times that there is so much to be done);
- incorporating the entire age range in the planning and implementation of the program—that is, not neglecting the older or younger ones in the group (or those in the middle!);
- individualising the daily experience or program to match particular needs, interests and styles;

- using the observations, insights and knowledge of parents and working in collaboration with them;
- giving priority to the social-emotional needs of children at this age, especially the need for attachment and security.

For babies and toddlers, play is a way of being. Adults working with this age group need to remind themselves and each other about what is important in the lives and experiences of these youngest children.

The best thing a caregiver can do is to enjoy the world and how it works, and share that pleasure with the child: looking at the infinite variety in nature and machines, humans and animals, and marvelling. The smoothness of a stone, the bumpiness of a piece of bark, the gold leaf with red veins, the boiling, whistling kettle, and the mist on the window are all daily encounters with science, as are dropping a spoon, sliding down an inclined surface, filling a bucket and pushing a table.

Children can learn from everything. Observe them, respond to their interests and explorations, play with them, support them and enjoy them. When caregivers have fun and take delight in play, children experience the joy of being human (Greenman & Stonehouse 1997, pp. 234–5).

For further thought and discussion

1. Fiona makes the point that 'babies and toddlers probably prefer fewer changes and surprises than we think'. Reflect on the changes you make to the environment where there are babies and toddlers. Do you think that you might be making changes too often? How will you know?
2. Consider the code that Fiona and Darlene use in planning for children's play. Would you be able to include PI (parent-initiated) planning? Do you ask families to tell you, on an ongoing basis, about their child's interests?
3. If you are a staff member working with babies and toddlers, or undertaking a field placement with this age group, try using the code Fiona and Darlene suggest as a basis for your planning. Ask families about their child's interests and incorporate their responses into your program.
4. Consider how you can incorporate play into the many routines that are important in babies' and toddlers' days. List some possible ways to achieve this.

5. What are the roles suggested in this chapter as being important for adults working with babies and toddlers? Do you agree with them? Are you, for example, 'excited' by the activities of young children?
6. Consider the philosophy of the service in which you are working, or doing your field experience. Is this philosophy reflected in practice?

Reference

Greenman, J. & Stonehouse, A. 1997, *Prime Times: A Handbook of Excellence in Infant and Toddler Care*, Addison–Wesley Longman, Melbourne.

Chapter 12

Persona dolls: the effects on attitudes and play

Kerry Bosisto and Anne Howard

Main Editor's interview with Kerry and Anne

I began by mentioning to Kerry and Anne that some people may question the inclusion of a chapter on persona dolls in a book about play. They both looked somewhat puzzled, and Kerry responded, 'but persona dolls are about play'.

Kerry: I guess we introduce persona dolls somewhat differently to the way other staff might. Some staff, I know, choose to keep the persona dolls for just the times they use them with children. When the teacher isn't using a doll it might be kept high on a shelf, for example. We wanted the children to play with them and take them home. We believe that in this way there will be greater acceptance of the dolls and potentially, therefore, of diversity. This extends to the families too. The families agree to children taking them home and the play at home can lead to discussions about diversity. The dolls are often central to children's play.

Elizabeth: Can you give me an example of how the dolls are incorporated into the play?

Anne: The dolls go everywhere with the children. Cubbies are built with, and for, the dolls, trees are climbed with them tucked under an arm, 'restaurants' are visited. Long Long (a Chinese doll) went home for a visit to a Chinese family and came back with his own miniature chopsticks and bowl so that he can use familiar eating implements when visiting the 'restaurant' or 'home' area—and 'feel good', one of the children said.

Kerry (to Anne): Do you recall the time when Jennifer came to me obviously quite tense and called, 'Long Long saw a lizard! There's a lizard out there!' I went off to investigate and found quite a sleepy lizard that I patted. Jennifer was very frightened and was not in the least bit interested in touching the lizard. I asked if Long Long would like to touch it very gently. Jennifer said he would. After Long Long touched the lizard Jennifer did. That led to lots of talk, do you remember? We had a ranger come to the kindergarten too and talk about lizards and snakes, and what you should do if you see a snake. I remember that 'ranger play' became popular and Long Long featured very much in it.

Anne: I do remember that day. I remember the family's notes in the diary too when Long Long went home that night. But I must tell you the story of some play that happened the other day. I forgot to tell you, Kerry. That's what happens when we are so busy. I was watching Jeremy, Anna and Shahla in the home corner. They were deciding what they were going to do that day. Shahla said something like, 'I think we should take the children to the playground, Dad'. Jeremy responded, 'Don't forget that Yu Yu (an Aboriginal persona doll) is scared on the slippery dip. We mustn't make her go on it.' That type of comment gives us confirmation that our anti-bias approach is having an effect. The children have adopted the principles of anti-bias through their play with persona dolls and can empathise with a doll's feelings.

Kerry: I think generally children are more caring. We don't hear comments now such as, 'you can't come in here because you're a girl, or because you are black'. I know if anything like this was said to one of the dolls, the children would very quickly make comments such as 'that's not fair' and say why. I think they would do it with each other now, too.

Anne: We were a bit concerned that for a few days the black dolls were being discarded, left on the floor and not dressed. One of the children, who was playing with Yu Yu, said 'Yu Yu doesn't like the black dolls just lying on the floor and getting cold.' Yu Yu's response led to the black dolls being dressed and put to bed! (smiling) Wasn't that a wonderful tracksuit that was made for Yu Yu? You see, Yu Yu had gone home with one of the children and came back in a tracksuit in Aboriginal colours. It was at the time of the Olympics and the tracksuit matched Cathy Freeman's suit. That led to some children playing the Olympics, and including Yu Yu and some of the other dolls. I remember that play went on for a long time.

Kerry: Our children's families are generally very supportive of the anti-bias approach using the dolls—as you might gather. They help with resources such as packages with labels in different languages. The Iranian and Chinese families are particularly helpful. They are the larger group and we have bilingual assistants from the same backgrounds. They are very pleased to see their culture represented in a meaningful, everyday way. Some of the families send food back with the dolls, too, so we often have different food to try.

Anne: I think you'll enjoy reading some of the diary entries in this chapter!

Elizabeth: Do boys generally play more with persona dolls now that they can borrow them?

Anne: I think they do. They prefer to take the boy dolls home and many of them do. I haven't heard the boys being called names like 'sissy' if they do play with the dolls. Have you, Kerry?

Kerry: No, I haven't. I would have remembered, I think, because I would have talked to the children about that—or we would have used the dolls to talk about it. The girls use the dolls a great deal and the boys are beginning to. Once, when Henry went home with Peter he didn't want to carry the doll to the car, so his Mum did. When they came back on the Monday, Peter had the doll on his hip.

Elizabeth: I'm looking forward to reading your chapter, Anne and Kerry. What messages do you think the readers can take from it?

Kerry: We believe that it will be very helpful for anyone considering introducing persona dolls, particularly if they also read Ana Maria Hanley's chapter, 'Persona dolls' (in *The Anti-bias Approach in Early Childhood*).

Anne: Yes, and Kerryn Jones' new book (*Persona Dolls: Anti-Bias in Action*). But I will just say that before introducing persona dolls, staff need to understand the principles of the anti-bias approach and have a commitment to them. Staff also need to address their individual biases and develop a team approach to have a real impact.

Kerry: I agree. But I also like to think that people will just find the chapter interesting to read, even if they aren't introducing persona dolls. I think many people will find the outcomes interesting and see how the anti-bias philosophy fits with early childhood principles.

Anne: And remember, our advice is—these dolls are for playing! They're not just for story-telling and discussion but are an important part of the total program.

Introduction

In 1996 Kerry inspired the staff at J. B. Cleland Kindergarten in Adelaide to explore racial awareness within our centre. This was an area in which we were both interested and about which we were concerned. We felt there were signs of some racial bias occurring within it.

We were successful in our application for the Lillian de Lissa Action Research Scholarship. This scholarship is available to staff of the Department for Education and Children's Services working with children under five years old and holding a qualification in early childhood education. The Action Research Scholarship provides funding for the project. The project must be supervised by a staff member of a recognised early childhood education tertiary institution for the purpose of benefiting the professional development of the applicant and the early childhood profession.

Our research project was entitled 'Developing critical thinking skills in an anti-bias curriculum'. We wanted to look at anti-bias curriculum in a specific rather than a broader context and so focused on racial awareness, although many other valuable learning outcomes emerged. The book *Anti-Bias Curriculum: Tools for Empowering Young Children* by Louise Derman-Sparks and the Anti-Bias Curriculum Task Force identifies goals that assisted us, including developing critical thinking and standing up for oneself and others in the face of injustice.

Ramsey (1995) discusses how crucial it is in classrooms that are relatively homogenous to stretch and challenge children's ideas about the world. Teachers can plan activities to help children develop assertiveness and empathy, think about what is fair and unfair, and work together to change biased situations beyond individual interactions with peers.

Derman-Sparks (1994) reminds us that 'children are just as vulnerable to omissions as they are to inaccuracies and stereotypes. What isn't seen can be as powerful a contributor to attitudes as what is seen'. So by having predominantly white middle-class people being represented in books, pictures and puzzles means the real world is not represented.

In *Foundation Areas of Learning* (1996), a curriculum framework for three- to five-year-olds, critical thinking is described as enhancing problem solving and decision making. This framework describes the teacher's role, which includes:

- challenging assumptions and bias;
- encouraging children to review their actions or thoughts;
- posing challenging questions;
- eliciting different points of view for consideration;
- encouraging interaction, interchange of ideas and group discussion.

How we started

We consulted and were guided by a number of people who were knowledgeable and experienced in the area of anti-bias. Some became our support group and we met on a regular basis. We read the current literature and research in anti-bias, critical thinking and racial awareness. On reflection, in discussion with our support group, and through observing what was happening within our centre, we decided to explore the use of persona dolls.

We thought the idea of presenting issues via the dolls could be a useful way to encourage critical thinking. The dolls could also provide one-step-removed situations so we weren't saying these issues necessarily happened to someone at kindergarten, but still had the opportunity to address some of the racial issues we were aware of there. Through our scholarship funding we were able to purchase dolls and other anti-bias curriculum materials, as well as fund relief staff, so we could be released from teaching to implement this project.

Data collection

In 1995 we conducted a sociometric measure. Children were asked to look at individual photographs of other children within their kindergarten group and put them under headings (see Figure 12.1).

I like to play with . . .	I sometimes like to play with . . .	I don't like to play with . . .

Our aim was to look at social interaction (friendship) patterns between children. We discovered that children from non-English speaking backgrounds or from minority racial groups were more often selected in the 'don't like to play with' category. We suspected that this was not because these children were necessarily actively disliked, but rather that there were barriers contributing to the lack of social interaction. Further observation and collecting of anecdotes reinforced our initial concern that racial bias existed in the centre.

Steve chose a white bus ticket from the floor rather than any paint sample, skin-toned shades and said emphatically, 'No, not those. This is my colour.'

Two girls, waiting their turn at the swing, chanted to Ying Ying (Chinese–Australian) and Geela (Iranian–Australian) who were on the swing. At first they chanted about their names but this became more of a taunt and Ying Ying and Geela were obviously uncomfortable.

A boy said to two other boys (Chinese–Australian) as they approached the digging patch, 'No Chinkies allowed.'

Zak to Geela: 'Go away from here. We don't want any girls.'
Teacher: 'It's not fair to say that she can't play because she's a girl.'
Zak: 'I mean we don't want any brown skin here—only white skin.'
Teacher: 'That's not fair. That's her skin colour and she can't change her skin.'
Zak: 'I wish she could.'

We randomly selected 15 children to become our focus group to work with throughout the action research project. We interviewed each of our sample group before and after our intervention program using the persona dolls. Pre-testing included:

• reading a multicultural story, 'Marty and Mei-Ling' or 'Cleversticks';
• showing a selection of multi-racial photographs of children.

'Marty and Mei-Ling' is a story about Mei-Ling, a new girl in Marty's class who feels that everyone is making fun of her because she is different. Marty finds himself in the same situation when he becomes lost in a crowd where everyone is speaking differently to him. Mei-Ling comes to Marty's rescue and they become good friends.

In 'Cleversticks', Ling Sun decides he doesn't like school as there are too many things others can do that he can't. One day he discovers something very special that he can do that others can't and enjoys showing everyone how to use chopsticks. His friends then help him with the things he couldn't do, and Ling Sun decides that school isn't so bad after all.

We asked all the children a number of questions to elicit their awareness of race, colour, permanence, self-identification and their preferences for playmates. Some patterns began to emerge:

- Children knew little about what it meant to be Chinese. Although they could identify them in pictures, they often had no answer to, 'How do you know?' or 'What do you know about Chinese people?'
- Self-identification was generally linked to skin colour—for example, 'I'm white'. Children from Iranian, Chinese or English backgrounds were very definite and quick to label themselves.

Children's reasons for choosing others with whom to play were linked to their having:

- the same hair—colour, length and style;
- the same gender—as in 'I only like to play with girls';
- similar clothing—for example, 'I like to play with her. She's got pretty clothes'—and similar facial expressions.

When considering the multi-racial photographs, children did not often choose a dark-skinned child as someone they would play with. When asked, 'could you play with this child?' some said, 'no'. Their reasons were either, 'I don't know' or 'his skin is too dark'. At the centre children have limited exposure to dark-skinned people and this may have influenced their responses.

There was a definite link between colour and emotion. Examples include:

- 'I might play only with people with white skin, but no girls.'
- 'Like your skin. Good colour!'
- 'No! His skin is too dark.'
- 'My favourite colour is white.'
- 'I don't like that skin. It's a bit too much dark. Don't like it dark. It makes my body hurt.'

- 'I don't like black skin. It makes me go sea-sick. It makes me go all funny and wobbly.'

Our findings were consistent with other research. Ramsey (1995) notes that the role that race plays in children's perceptions of themselves and others depends in part on their majority or minority status in their local community. This was evident in our study where children from minority groups had a more definite knowledge of their racial background.

However, our findings differed in a number of other ways. Non-racial attributes dominated children's choices of possible friendships when they didn't know those in the photographs, whereas in the sociometric study it was apparent that children from minority racial groups were least preferred as playmates. The different methodology in each interview may have contributed to children feeling that in direct questioning 'the right answer' was required, whereas in a non-verbal choice they were not required to justify or explain themselves.

Derman-Sparks and the ABC Task Force (1989) state that while skin colour is a frequent focus of interest among preschoolers, they also get confused about racial group names, the actual colour of their skin and why two people with different skin tones are considered part of the same group. Ramsey (1995) also notes that preschoolers are often inconsistent when asked whom they look like, and frequently make distinctions on non-racial attributes such as hairstyle and clothing.

Derman-Sparks and the ABC Task Force (1989) discuss the continual reinforcement of black being equated with dirt in our society and not being valued, whereas white is clean and valued. Derman-Sparks (1994) also states that racism results in white children developing fears about people different from themselves.

Interviews with parents

We interviewed the parents of each of the children we had focused on to find out what they believed was their children's awareness of race and what contact they, as a family, had with people of a different background to their own. Most said that their children did notice differences but saw themselves as the same as others: 'Children accept all children. It doesn't make any difference if they are black, green or purple.' Some families mentioned *Sesame Street* as having an influence on their child's racial awareness.

We sensed that some children had learned 'middle-class politeness' in referring to other children in a seemingly accepting manner while their body language and behaviour in a social setting were less accepting. This is consistent with the findings of Derman-Sparks and ABC Task Force (1989).

Staff involvement

Each staff member, including bilingual support workers employed to support children maintain their first language and develop skills in speaking English while enhancing cultural awareness within the kindergarten, were asked to complete an anti-bias checklist (included at the end of this chapter) in relation to our kindergarten. This yielded valuable information and changes were implemented as a result. More information for first contact at the centre in languages other than English on the community newsboard and display of staff photographs and names are two examples. All staff were kept up-to-date with the action research project, and the bilingual support workers were involved in information-sharing about persona dolls among families whose first language was not English.

Persona dolls should reflect the reality of today's society—for example, single parents—while still respecting the family values of all cultural groups. Our Chinese–Australian bilingual support worker told us, for example, that it would be more culturally appropriate from the Chinese point of view to mention that Long Long's (Chinese persona doll) father lived in Sydney, leaving it open as to whether the parents had separated, since divorce is generally not accepted within the Chinese community.

The project has heightened staff's awareness of such issues and challenged biases through staff discussions and sharing of ideas.

Parent involvement

This included extensive information-sharing over a ten-week term, and involved:

- showing the film *The Colour of Fear* which depicted eight men from both minority and majority cultural backgrounds spending a weekend workshop together sharing their experiences and perceptions of racism;

- providing newsletters with frequent updates on our research as well as snippets of current research or media releases that we felt would provide information and help raise parents' awareness about anti-bias curriculum and children's developmental stages in relation to racism;
- requesting feedback on any aspect of the action research project and program at the kindergarten as well as any information or support that parents could supply;
- providing a careful and extensive introduction to the concept of persona dolls;
- encouraging parents to use the persona dolls' diaries; for example, writing in a doll's diary when that doll visited their home and describing activities in which the doll participated.

Structure of sessions

Each week at the same time one of us took the sample group for an extended group activity time lasting approximately 30–40 minutes, while the other videotaped the session. We felt it was important to establish a 'group-feel' so we started with some 'get to know you' activities as a warm-up and emphasised the special group aspect of sharing the dolls. We established a climate of mutual support and trust by making some ground rules at the first session so that we all felt secure; for example, no put-downs and no laughing at what others said. At subsequent sessions children were reminded of these rules.

The warm-up activity was always interactive and would often involve children finding another child with similar or different physical characteristics while staff would facilitate comparative discussion in an affirming, open manner; for example, 'Yes, you have a short nose and your nose is narrow.' These comparisons invited frank and non-biased discussion on physical attributes and helped children describe differences in a matter-of-fact, non-judgmental way. They also helped staff demonstrate a lack of inhibition and overcome their initial embarrassment in discussing differences openly.

Having started with group work, the staff would then produce a doll. We had four dolls: Long Long (Chinese–Australian), Sima (Iranian–Australian), Henry (Anglo–Australian with a visual impairment) and Yu-Yu (Aboriginal). Each doll's story was read out from their diary which we had written and which outlined the doll's age, facial characteristics, family composition, cultural and religious background, household location, family interests and activities.

An extract from Sima's diary reads:

Sima's story

My name is Sima and I live with my mother, father, brother and sister. I call my mother Momman and my father Baba. We live in a flat. It hasn't got as much room as my house in Iran so I share my bedroom with my big sister. My Baba works at a place called Waite. He is learning about agriculture (plants and farm animals). My Momman looks after our flat and is a teacher on the weekend at a Persian school. My big brother and big sister go to the big school. I go to kindergarten. Soon I will go to the big school with my brother and sister.

We used to live in Iran, but now we live in Australia. Iran is a long way from here. We came here in a big plane. It took us two days. We had to stay in Malaysia for one night. We will stay in Australia for four years then we will go back to Iran. We have lived in our flat for one year.

I forgot to tell you my family's names. My sister's name is Sare and my brother's name is Saba.

My favourite toy is my doll called Shashad. I have a little bed that she sleeps in and a blanket to wrap her to keep her warm. My favourite food is Poloo which is rice and Kabab which is meat on skewers. My favourite TV program is *Play School*. My favourite thing that I like to do is visiting our friends with my Momman. Our friend has a little baby. I look after her when my mother talks to the baby's mother. They talk and drink tea. Last weekend we went to the park for a picnic with our friends. We played on the swings and the slippery dip with the other children.

The diary and story remain with the doll for its time in the centre to ensure consistency. All anecdotes are recorded in the book along with children's responses at group time. Interspersed with the entries are the daily recordings written by the families outlining what happened with the doll at their house (play, meals, bath and bedtime routines, for example).

When staff presented an incident involving one of the dolls for group discussion, the children were asked how they would feel in the doll's position and then brainstorm some strategies to resolve the incident. Children were also asked what they could do to help the persona doll—what words they could use to the other children. The children empathised with the doll who had been treated in a biased way and, as four-year-olds have a strong sense of justice, they quickly became involved in a discussion of fairness.

Questions were framed to elicit information and encourage further thinking without staff judging the responses right or wrong. Later analysis would reveal the appropriateness of their suggestions and how staff needed to trust the process rather than hastily label it as biased. All ideas were accepted initially and later scrutinised for fairness and 'workability'. Rather than decide immediately on a course of action for the doll to try we often left the ideas in abeyance for a period of time, ideally until the next day. We then came back to it with the statement, 'I've been thinking about the suggestion' (without naming the person who offered it) 'for example, "to run away and hide". How do you think that would help Sima work it out and how would she feel when she was hiding?'

We would also reconsider the suggestions in the light of possible consequences (such as safety or others' feelings). Sometimes a suggestion was to retaliate with a counter-bias; for example, if the children said Long Long is a girl because his hair is long, he could say the girls are boys. We could then discuss people's identity and the need to respect that of each individual. Some explicit teaching of social skills occurred with modelling of responses.

Findings

The following observations were made during the persona doll project when comparing the interviews that were seven weeks apart:

- There was more general awareness of Chinese–Australian children attending the centre, although mostly they were still not mentioned. Chinese people were seen as living in China and two children in the study group were not referred to as 'Chinese' because they spoke fluent English—despite the fact that they did speak to each other in Mandarin and their parents were often overhead speaking Mandarin.
- There was more awareness of detail when children noticed Chinese writing on a child's T-shirt in a picture. Previously only the Chinese–Australian children had pointed the writing out.
- In neither interview did children have names for children with dark skin. One called them 'Indian' as we had recently been on an excur-

sion to the Indian Village at a school in Adelaide, but most referred to them as black or brown. One child said 'boong'. No-one used the term 'Aboriginal' or 'African–American'.

- Most came to realise that skin colour is unchangeable. Some children said every skin is the same colour; others said it could change when you grow up. Some children of Chinese descent said it might change and referred to their palms and the different colour on the backs of their hands.
- Children of Chinese–Australian and Iranian–Australian backgrounds showed similar levels of anxiety as Anglo-Saxon children in regard to playing with children with dark skin. For example, 'no, his skin is too dark', 'he's a tiny little bit dark' or 'can't play with black skin'.
- Iranian–Australian children in the study group had limited English; however, they more consistently recognised and labelled children in the pictures as Chinese. Ying Ying was referred to as a Chinese–Australian child attending the kindergarten, yet Win and Andrew were overlooked even though their physical appearances were distinctly Chinese. Ying Ying spoke very little English whereas Win and Andrew spoke mostly English.
- 'Black' was often referred to as different.

We decided to run a second sociometric study (which did not consist of entirely the same group but had a similar racial/cultural composition) and this revealed a marked difference. The children of non-English speaking backgrounds were more integrated and accepted by others (chosen as 'like to play with'). We believe that their inclusion in the study group and work by staff in addressing their social needs helped account for this difference.

While the results of the formal pre- and post-tests were similar in many respects, children of non-English speaking backgrounds became more confident in asserting their ethnicity, and generally all children were more comfortable discussing skin colour, eye shape and so on. The staff found that families had more contact with diverse cultural/racial groups than we had assumed (two families had Aboriginal friends or relations) and could affirm these with their children. The staff were more aware of the subtle aspects of bias and became more confident in recognising bias in themselves, challenging it among each other, and discussing it with parents.

The persona dolls provided daily opportunities for open discussion of race and bias, and families were encouraged to be involved with the persona dolls in a non-threatening way. They could choose to borrow them and write about the time they shared. The spin-off for boys was their attitude to the dolls. We found that boys had a definite preference for the boy-dolls whereas girls borrowed both equally. This showed a need for gender-balance among persona dolls in a centre.

Family responses

While anti-bias is the main focus for having persona dolls as part of our curriculum, families relate to them as special visitors to their homes. Examples of diary excerpts written by families follow.

In the name of God. Hello, my name is Leila. I am Iranian. Now I live with my father, mother and brother in Adelaide City. We rent a two-bedroom flat. My father is a Ph.D. student. He studies at the Adelaide University (Waite Institute). My mother is a housewife. My brother is five years older than me. He studies at Linden Park Primary School in Year Five. This is the third term that I come to kindergarten. I love kindergarten so much and enjoy the kindy programs.

Today I was very happy because Sima was with me. I had been invited to my friend Nazanin's house for lunch today. I went there with Sima. We had lunch at Nazanin's house. We played many games after lunch. My mother came to Nazanin's house this afternoon. We came back to our house with Sima. I watched TV at my home. I like kids' programs especially *Play School* and cartoons. I ate dinner at evening and came to bed very soon. Sima slept beside me. I enjoyed all the time because I like Sima and everyone that organised this nice program for me.

Leila 5/6/1996
(Written in Persian and translated by Shahla
Pakrou, bilingual support worker)

Long Long went to Aaron's place to stay overnight. Aaron took Long Long home in his mum's car and happily introduced Long Long to his grandmother and baby brother. After having Long Long's favourite noodles for lunch, Aaron's mum took the two boys out shopping. On the way back home Aaron took Long Long to his previous address to see how things were packed up to be shipped to Hong Kong before the family move over there in July. Aaron told mum that Long Long was from Hong Kong too and that was why he could speak both English and Chinese like Aaron did. Aaron spoke with Long Long in Chinese all the time as it is his mother tongue.

After shopping, Long Long and Aaron went home and watched *Play School* and *Sesame Street*. Aaron then started his daily exercise on Chinese writing and taught Long Long some simple Chinese words. When Aaron's dad came home from work, Aaron told him enthusiastically that he had Long Long home for a visit.

At the dinner table, Long Long received a warm welcome from Aaron's family and was treated a traditional Chinese meal. Aaron even gave Long Long a pair of chopsticks to take with him as Long Long may not be able to find chopsticks in other families.

After dinner and a brief play time, the two boys enjoyed a bubble bath together. Aaron carefully helped Long Long to undress, bath and shampoo, understanding that he should help to look after younger kids. They then both went to bed early as they have to get up early tomorrow for the visit to Indian village.

Bye, Long Long—please come again.

Aaron 12/6/1996

Today Henry slept over at Travis' house as tomorrow morning they are both going to the eye specialist. After kindy we went home and had lunch with Daniel and Jasmine who visited for the afternoon. We played most of the afternoon then went to swimming lessons. It was then time for tea and a bath. Daddy read a bedtime story and Travis made a special bed for Henry at the end of his.

Next morning we were up early and off to the eye specialist. Travis' eyes were tested and have improved 50 per cent although he needs to wear his patch for another month. We also discussed Henry's problem with Dr Munt. He said he was a good boy for wearing his glasses but does need to wear the patch a little more, then his sight would also improve. Then it was time for kindy.

Travis 30/10/1996

Yu Yu came for a sleepover at Alison's house on Monday night. Alison was very excited at having a friend to play. When we all got home, Alison introduced Yu Yu to her brother Hugh and then they all had a swing, but first they had to clean the swing as it was so wet and dirty from the wet weekend.

After the swing, everyone had some lunch while they watched a little of the closing ceremony of the Olympic Games. I explained to Alison why Cathy Freeman had the same colour skin as Yu Yu so Alison then wanted to go and run her own 400 metre race.

Later in the afternoon Sam and Rory came to play while Alison made sure Yu Yu was well looked after. When we went to the playground Alison put Yu Yu down for a sleep after her exhausting afternoon, followed by a lovely warm bath.

> Yu Yu shared Alison's bed and they both slept very well. In the morning, Alison got Yu Yu dressed into her tracksuit while we talked about the Aboriginal flag and its colours. After a breakfast of Weet-Bix the girls were ready for kindergarten with Alison a little sad that Yu Yu had to go home. We hope she can come again.
>
> Alison 5/8/1996

While some family members did write down responses to incidents of bias in the diary, they were mostly the families whose children had been in the sample group with a more personal environment—as in the case of Simon, who said, 'I know just how Long Long felt because that happened to me once.' Members of the larger, staff-led group who had only limited interactions with the dolls reported on the overnight events in their household rather than incidents of bias.

In later months, staff found that maintaining the presence of four dolls and their stories was time-consuming and that the children's interest flagged if we didn't keep up regular involvement with the dolls ourselves. This year, each of our three staff have 'adopted' a doll and work weekly with it in a regular group who have priority in borrowing the doll. We expect that this will provide a more consistent program, greater borrowing and closer involvement for each child in our anti-bias curriculum. While further developing staff skills in addressing what we now consider an essential component of the preschool experience, we may even be brave enough to infiltrate our local Junior Primary and send a persona doll to school!

Conclusion

Children in our study may not be termed racist in their behaviours and attitudes as their comments are consistent with their developmental stage. While as early childhood practitioners we need to be considerate of the children's limited experience and knowledge of race, anecdotal evidence shows that the misinformation they receive from various sources (such as media, playground and family) must be challenged at this critical stage of attitudinal development. Further, we do not consider it adequate to merely address issues as they arise; rather, we must take a proactive approach within an anti-bias environment. As Derman-Sparks states, 'our aim is to promote critical thinkers and activists who can work for social change and participate in creating a caring culture in a world of differences' (Derman-Sparks 1994, p. 69).

Through the use of persona dolls as described in this chapter, we believe that we have gone a long way towards meeting this aim. We encourage you to think about introducing persona dolls into your service as a way of teaching children to accept differences. An anti-bias approach is not only about establishing an environment that reflects differences in the resources used, but also about shaping prevailing attitudes. By using persona dolls with children, and involving their families, attitudes can be challenged and in many instances changed. This change means we are on the path to creating, as Derman-Sparks puts it, that 'caring culture'.

For further thought and discussion

1. If you plan to introduce persona dolls, what preparation would you as staff do to ensure that anti-bias principles are followed?
2. How would you involve and inform parents about the anti-bias curriculum and how persona dolls relate to it? How would you approach parental concerns about an anti-bias curriculum (for instance, raising children's awareness unnecessarily)?
3. How would you handle or confront bias by children at play?
4. How would you raise your own awareness of bias?
5. Use the anti-bias checklist which follows to highlight bias that may exist in your setting.
6. Discuss with your staff team how you might approach a situation where the black-skinned dolls are thrown aside on the floor without clothes and only white-skinned dolls are being played with.
7. Discuss the difference between an anti-bias and a multicultural curriculum.
8. How would you incorporate anti-bias activities into the daily curriculum planning?
9. Find ways to engage children in critical thinking and planning and carrying out 'activism' activities appropriate to their developmental levels, cultural backgrounds and interests.
10. Think about forming a support group to meet with, share resources and provide encouragement in your own development of an anti-bias approach.

Cross-Cultural, Anti-Bias Centre Environment Checklist

Entrance/Lobby Areas

- Are there posters, notices or other information displays and welcome notices in relevant community languages?
- Are there multilingual information leaflets for parents (eg Department of Health)?
- Is there space somewhere in the centre devoted to the interests and cultural backgrounds of the children's parents?
- Are there photographs and other pictures reflecting the various backgrounds of the children, parents and staff attractively displayed?
- Do the pictures and other displays reflect the cultural diversity of Australia?

Dramatic Play Area

In addition to the usual furniture, household utensils and other items, does the area include:

- Utensils commonly used by people from a variety of cultures (eg wok, chopsticks)?
- Furniture common to a variety of cultures (eg low tables with cushions for sitting, mats for bedding)?
- Clothing and hats worn by people from a variety of cultures (everyday, for work, festivals and holidays)?
- Food packages (eg tins, boxes) that have labels in other languages as well as English (eg those found in ethnic food shops, Chinatown)?
- Puppets that have clothing, skin tones and features representing different cultures?
- Girl and boy dolls with features, skin and hair colour, and varieties of clothing to represent different cultural and ethnic groups?
- A selection of homemade and purchased boy and girl dolls with different kinds of disabilities (eg cast on leg) to represent different ethnic groups?
- Pictures such as posters or photos to show families from different cultures in typical situations (eg feeding children)?
- Pictures of women and men at work, both 'blue collar' roles (eg factory worker, repair person) as well as 'white collar' roles (eg teacher, doctor)?

- Pictures of elderly people from different backgrounds doing different activities?
- Pictures of disabled people from various backgrounds with their families, in recreational activities or work roles? (Be careful not to use images that portray people with disabilities as passive and dependent.)
- Artefacts or decorations reflecting traditional colours and patterns of various cultures (eg mats, rugs, wall hangings, sculptures)?
- Baby-carriers or cradles from different cultures?
- Full-length and hand-mirrors?

Art/Craft Area

- Are art/craft activities set up outdoors as well as indoors? Is the area set up away from busy traffic areas?
- Is the area well lit?
- In addition to the usual art/craft material do you frequently provide: finger paint, crayons, textas, coloured chalk, easel paper, drawing paper and paper for collage?
- Do you provide play dough in a spectrum of brown shades from light to dark brown, and mixed paint for easel painting in different skin tones?
- Do you display any designs or patterns representing different cultures (eg Aboriginal motifs, Pacific Islander designs)?
- Do you display crafts common to different cultures (eg weaving, woodwork, pottery, enamelware, embroidery)?
- Is there opportunity for children to work with natural materials (eg twigs, stones, earth, leaves, clay)?

Library Area

- Is the area set up in a quiet place away from heavy traffic?
- Is the area attractive and inviting?
- How many of the books are written in English?
- How many of the books are bilingual? Do the illustrations in some of the books reflect the children's environment and experience?
- Do some of the books positively reflect diversity of gender roles, ethnic and cultural backgrounds, special needs and disabilities, and a range of occupations and ages?
- Do the illustrations and content of some of the books positively depict different cultural groups living their daily lives, solving issues relevant to young children, as well as having celebrations?

- Do the books present accurate images and information or do they present the 'I is for Indian' stereotyped alphabet book approach?
- Do the books positively depict various family lifestyles, income and religious backgrounds? (Beware of books picturing only two-parent families.)
- Are the books available for loan by families in English and community languages?

Block Area

- Is the area large enough for children to play constructively?
- Is the area located away from quiet activities?
- Do the supplementary block toys include scaled down multi-ethnic figures of people, trees and animals?
- Are there posters, illustrations or photographs of people, buildings and transport typical of your area?
- Are there frequent displays of posters and pictures reflecting different cultures and lifestyles?

Puzzles/Games/Manipulative Equipment

- Do the materials develop concepts and skills in various ways?
- Do the materials include:

spatial relationships	memory
sequencing	matching
counting	association
classification	

- Do some of the illustrations on the materials reflect the children's environment (eg rural/urban)?
- Do some of the illustrations depict diversity in culture, ethnicity, gender and physical abilities?

Music

- Does some of the material have words printed in English and other languages?
- Are the materials clearly visible and easily reached?
- Are there records or cassettes of music from different cultures?
- Do the children have access to musical instruments typical of different cultures?
- Do the children have the opportunity to see and hear music and dances of different cultural groups?

- Are dances and musical rhythmic games taught that are typical of different cultures?
- Are children taught finger-plays, rhymes and songs in languages other than English?

Outdoor Area

In addition to the equipment commonly found in outdoor areas, do you have any of the following:

- Music of different cultures to accompany children jumping on, say, a board?
- Permanent outdoor music centres containing Indian bells, wind chimes or chime bars with different musical tones?
- Do you sometimes have cubbies made from palm fronds, branches of trees or canvas?
- Do you ever make mud bricks?

For dramatic play do you have or arrange for any of the following:

- Outdoor markets with mats and baskets?
- Low tables and cushions?
- Preparing, cooking and eating food outdoors (eg cooking in an underground oven)?
- Making animal enclosures, or hammocks for babies/children/dolls?
- Exploring tools used by people with various special needs (eg wheelchairs, crutches, braces, canes, thick glasses, hearing aids)?

Sand and Water Play

- In addition to the usual equipment, is there a variety of materials commonly used by other cultures (eg wok, steamers, strainers, Lebanese cake moulds)?
- Is there an opportunity to make use of sand, earth and clay within different cultural traditions?

Woodwork

- Is there a woodwork bench available?
- Are the rules for using the tools clearly defined and enforced?
- Are there frequent displays of wooden objects and pictures typical of your area and of different cultures?

Centres of Interest

- Are there frequent displays of wooden objects and pictures typical of different cultures (eg buildings, bridges, forms of transport)?
- Are there pictures, posters or artefacts displayed of events that have special significance to the children and parents in your centre?
- Are these displays and pictures used in storytime and discussions?
- Are families asked to help in setting up displays to provide information or translating notices and so on?
- Do menus reflect the food habits of children attending the centre?
- Are alternative foods available to children when foods are not allowed for religious, cultural or health reasons?
- Do the cooking experiences in the playroom encourage children to experiment with foods other than those familiar to them?

Staff

- Are all the staff encouraged to learn more about the cultures in the centre as well as other cultures?
- Are bilingual and bicultural staff employed?
- Are bilingual staff encouraged to use their languages with the children throughout the day?
- Do staff have opportunities to participate in ongoing in-service about cross-cultural anti-bias issues?

Source: Hopson, E. 1990, *Valuing Diversity: Implementing a Cross-Cultural, Anti-bias Approach in Early Childhood Programmes*, Lady Gowrie Child Centre, Sydney. Reprinted with permission.

References

Ashley, B. 1992, *Cleversticks*, Harper Collins, London.

Cummings, P. & Smith, C. 1996, *Marty and Mei-Ling*, Random House, Sydney.

Department for Education and Children's Services 1996, *Foundation Areas of Learning: A Curriculum Framework*, Adelaide.

Derman-Sparks, L. 1994, 'Empowering children to create a caring world in a world of differences', *Childhood Education*, vol. 70, no. 2, pp. 66–71.

Derman-Sparks, L. & the ABC Task Force 1989, *Anti-Bias Curriculum: Tools for Empowering Young Children*, National Association for the Education of Young Children, Washington DC.

Hanley, A. 1995, 'Persona dolls' in Creaser, B. and Dau, E. (eds), *The Anti-Bias Approach in Early Childhood*, HarperEducational, Sydney.

Jones, K. and Mules, R. 1997, *Persona Dolls: Anti-Bias in Action*, Lady Gowrie Child Centre, Sydney.

Ramsey, P. 1995, 'Growing up with the contradictions of race and class', *Young Children*, Sept.

Chapter 13

'I can be playful too': the adult's role in children's socio-dramatic play

Elizabeth Dau

Introduction

I decided that the chapter I would write for this book would be about the adult's role in children's play. I mentioned this to a friend, Louise, who asked, 'have you done a mind map?' I responded, 'what is a mind map?' Louise said, 'let's do one now', and with two other friends and over a cup of coffee, we compiled a mind map. Louise is a much sought-after speaker. She gives all her talks using mind maps and was a committed player in this process. I had first encountered mind-mapping, I realised, when I attended a talk by Dr Elizabeth Jones in Darwin. She called it 'webbing'.

From this exercise, which was done on a large sheet of brown paper, I was surprised by what is required of the adult committed to children's play. One chapter is not long enough to cover the topics we elicited, but I will address a number of them including the impor- tance of observations, planning the program, real-life experiences, time, prop boxes and materials. You may choose to research others yourself.

The styles and modes of approach to learning that children adopt include those of dramatist, explorer and spectator.

Dramatist

Dramatist children play predominantly in the pretend mode and take on roles seemingly with ease. They can become mummy, police officer, doctor or zoo-keeper and 'at the most complex level can imagine the props and scenes with little or no materials' (Creaser 1990(a), pp. 3– 4).

Explorer

Explorer children may also be described as builders or constructors. They are children who, according to Creaser, 'see their environment as a laboratory in which they can experiment' (Creaser 1990[a], pp. 3–4). They like investigating and finding out how things work. Only when the last block is laid, or the last piece of the puzzle fits, have they have completed their task.

Spectator

Children who are spectators often watch the play, listen and sometimes make comments. This frequently causes concern in adults, but it may be that these children simply have a different mode of learning. Weininger (cited in Creaser 1990[b]) separates pretending and imagining, and suggests that the imaginary may still be happening for the spectator but the pretend mode is obscure.

The approach to learning addressed in this chapter is that of the dramatist, and it focuses on socio-dramatic play—dramatic play in its most developed form. In dramatic play, children take on roles; this becomes socio-dramatic play when 'the theme is elaborated in cooperation with others both in action and verbally. Some of the verbal interaction is imitation of adult talk and an integral part of the role playing; some is verbal substitution of objects' (Smilansky 1968, p. 7).

Socio-dramatic play should be available to all children, although there will be a group of children for whom it is the preferred way of learning. For these children, it is imperative that there are many opportunities for play and that staff support and resource their play. Evidence suggests that in most services we cater well for the child who is an explorer, but less well for the child who is a dramatist. Why should this be so? I think that staff find it very difficult to relinquish their power and allow children to be in charge, to give them the freedom to plan, construct and play and to make time for the types of experiences that Ria gave her 'builders' (described in the section on real-life experiences, later in this chapter).

Being a good early childhood teacher is, I believe, about:

• instigating children's play (as Chris did in the story in the Introduction);
• elaborating on children's own self-directed play themes;
• providing the impetus for children's play (as Ria did).

Sometimes this may mean that as a teacher you are:

- a resource person—a provider of the set, materials and ambience;
- an observer;
- a supporter;
- an interactor, co-player or mediator;
- a recorder, at children's requests or for evaluation and further planning.

Observing children's socio-dramatic play

> How do we know what children are doing and learning? We watch and listen to them, paying attention to details of their action and language. (Jones & Reynolds 1997, p. 78)

Jones and Reynolds also suggest that 'informal and systematic observation during independent activity, including play, is the primary tool in early childhood education' (Jones & Reynolds 1997, p. 78). I'd like to replace 'is' with 'should be' in their quote, however. While most teachers plan on the basis of observations, others don't see play—socio-dramatic play—as worthy of observation. If they did observe, listen, and take note of what early childhood educators and researchers have to say, they would understand just how complex children's play is and what a wealth of information can be gained from it about their development.

Observations of children's socio-dramatic play are usually based on written records of the child's language and activities. These observations can lead to a much better understanding of children, as well as giving staff many clues about how to extend, initiate and plan for children's play.

There are a number of formats that can be used to record observations of children. One that is particularly useful for observing children's socio-dramatic play is shown in Figure 13.1.

It is not, of course, either possible or necessary in a busy service to observe all children each week, so many staff identify 'focus children' each week to ensure that all children are subject to systematic observation. An example of play that has been observed and recorded using this format is shown in Figure 13.2, where Ruth was one of the focus children that week.

What can we learn from this single observation of Ruth in play with Carly? We can decode and 'make best guesses' about Ruth and

FOCUS CHILD: ....
AGE: ....
SEX: ....
TIME: ....
DATE: ....

SCENE (Theme or topic of play)	SCRIPT (Focus child and responses as much as possible)	ACTION (What is happening)	SOCIAL SET (Number, sex and age of the players)

Figure 13.1: Format of a chart to record children's socio–dramatic play

SCENE (Theme or topic of play)	SCRIPT (Focus child and responses as much as possible)	ACTION (What is happening)	SOCIAL SET (Number, sex and age of the players)
Hairdressing on verandah area	*Ruth:* will you comb my hair, so I look beautiful? Can you do my hair like that picture? I like my hair like that. I had beautiful long curly hair, I did. I went to the hairdresser and she cut my hair. Now I have short hair. It is cool. But now it is getting longer again. *Carly:* Do you want water on it? *Ruth:* Yes, you need water to make your hair soft. My hair is soft. *Carly:* I'll just put some on, okay! *Ruth:* Yes. Let's go and play with the play dough. *Carly:* Not yet, I haven't finished. *Ruth:* I'll do your hair.	Ruth is sitting at hairdressing table. Carly is combing her hair, very intent on looking at her hair while she is doing it. Ruth is talking while she is looking at the posters in front of her of different hair styles.	Carly 3.2

Figure 13.2: Completed chart of a focus child's socio-dramatic play

reach some conclusions, but these will need to be confirmed by further observations. From observing the hairdressing scene we can, for example, conclude that Ruth:

- can take on a role;
- has well-developed language skills, can express needs and ideas, and respond appropriately to questions using reasoning;
- understands the concept of opposite (short–long) and has a concept of what is beautiful;
- is able to maintain an imaginative environment;
- is cooperative (shown by her agreement to maintain the play rather than move to the play dough).

You could also choose to observe children and record the outcomes using the elements of socio-dramatic play (for a description of one tool for evaluating socio-dramatic play, see Smilansky & Shefatya 1990, pp. 237–55). These elements are:

- imitative role play—the child takes on a role and expresses it through language and action;
- make-believe objects are substituted for the real ones;
- make-believe with regard to actions and situations—verbal descriptions are substituted for real actions and situations;
- persistence in the play;
- interaction—there are at least two players interacting within the context of the play;
- verbal communication—there is some verbal interaction related to the play.

(Smilansky & Shefatya 1990, pp. 238–9)

Planning for socio-dramatic play

Program-planning is a complex task if all learning styles are taken into account. The program must ensure that play is available for both the explorers and the dramatists, that it includes children's interests and teacher-initiated experiences, and that it takes account of individual needs. Often several themes run concurrently with different small groups or pairs of children involved. The component of a weekly program that plans for dramatists might look something like that shown in Figure 13.3.

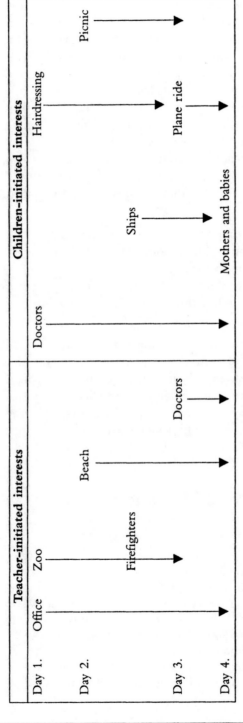

Figure 13.3: Example of a written plan for dramatists' play over a few days

You can see from this that the children's interest in hairdressing play has continued. The teacher observing Ruth, a focus child, has allowed this play to continue while adding more materials to the environment, perhaps to extend Ruth's play but also to involve others in the play. A few chairs have been arranged as a waiting area, and magazines in various languages are available for 'clients'. Meanwhile, other groups of dramatists are playing out several themes. You will notice that play also begins, continues or ends over the week. The hairdressing play continued while children were interested.

There are also teacher-initiated play environments established. There may be any number of reasons for teachers planning to initiate children's socio-dramatic play. Play environments may have been planned:

- as a follow-up, or precursor, to an excursion;
- to discover what children know about this theme;
- to extend children's play;
- as a possible play theme following the planned story reading;
- as a response to what one child was heard talking about.

You can see from the socio-dramatic play component of a teacher's weekly plan that play may be occurring in many areas of the environment both inside and out. A program like Chris's (see the Introduction) allows for greater flexibility in fostering children's socio-dramatic play. It allows for play indoors or outdoors depending on where the environment is set up or where it best suits children wanting to establish a socio-dramatic play theme.

The value of real-life experiences

Ria took a group of five children up the road to where some new houses were being built. On the way back to the centre one of the children suggested building his own house. Ria commented, 'To build a house it is good to have more than one person. We have seen lots of people today helping to build the houses. We saw carpenters, painters, plumbers and people laying bricks.'
'I can be a carpenter!' called one boy.
'My daddy's a painter. Can I paint?' one girl said.
Another said, 'I can build really good with the blocks so I'll help.'

Ria responded to the children's enthusiasm and suggested that the very large carton in the shed might be useful. She was also aware that there were other resources in the shed that the children might choose to use.

What followed was a very busy afternoon as the children worked cooperatively on designing and constructing a house—that is, until Ria heard an argument. On going over to investigate she heard one child say, 'But I *want* the house to be pink! I *want* it to be a Barbie house!' Ria asked about the colours of the houses that they lived in and eventually they reached a compromise: it would be painted red. After further discussion the children also agreed that after the house was finished it could belong to whomever they chose.

During the ensuing weeks, play continued around many different themes in the house they had built and in the surrounds. The excursion had captured the interest of all five children and many more joined in the socio-dramatic play that followed.

If we want children to engage in socio-dramatic play, the many advantages of which have been spelt out in other chapters, excursions can form the basis for play. Before children can build houses, they have to know what is needed and who will take part. Some children will already have a clear idea about this; others may have suggestions, such as the child whose father was a painter; and still others may have no idea at all, never having seen a house being built. Learning and understanding about a host of things connected to building came from this excursion, the subsequent creating of a house and the ensuing play. A great deal of other learning took place too—alongside the learning about building a house.

Children need real-life experiences such as this outing to see the houses being built, in order to help build their play:

> Just as children come from environments that will have accepted or rejected their socio-dramatic play, so also do they come from environments that may or may not have extended their experience. The real-life experiences for any young children can be expanded upon with activities such as a visit to the local fire-station, a walk in the park or an outing to the zoo. (Dau 1991, p. 77)

Children need different experiences at different ages. The children in the house-building story are all aged four and five. If you work with younger children, you might take them to places they may have already experienced, but in order to play the particular theme they need to see more. You might decide, for example, that children who have been playing mothers and fathers for some time could broaden this play. A trip to the local doctor might be planned in order to extend both their knowledge and their play.

Listen to the children. They will give you clues about what they are interested in, and the interests of one or two children can spread out to others. Play following an excursion can be encouraged without difficulty. Ria's comment about the large cardboard carton in the shed, and her knowledge that there were other materials available, indicated a support for the children's ideas. The play theme should never be compulsory, however. Those children who are interested will be the ones to gain from the experience.

Making time for socio-dramatic play

Here I feel that words frequently belie our actions. So often 'free play' is slotted into timetables for short periods by staff because it just 'fills this gap nicely'. Yet socio-dramatic play cannot happen in a few minutes of free play—children need time to initiate the play, negotiate roles, plan the play and often establish the environment.

I am reminded of a play episode I observed. This play, the teacher informed me later, continued over two weeks with various players moving in and out of the play and adjunct themes being developed.

The teacher had brought in two small fishing rods for the storeroom as a resource if needed. Two children immediately seized on the rods. Preparation for play then went on all morning while various children explored the use of the rods.

One child spent the morning looking at books and drawing fish. She then coloured in her drawings with a wonderful array of shades and cut them out. She created a whole variety of fish. Another two children built a 'lake' with outdoor blocks, and yet another put together a large floor puzzle of a crocodile. Meanwhile, children were also constructing more fishing lines with sticks and string. Only after all the preparation was completed did the play begin with initial negotiation of roles.

The child who had so carefully spent hours making the fish did not enter the play at all. She was an explorer. She was content to spend the time creating in order that others could play.

In sharp contrast to this, I recall another play episode I observed recently.

Teacher: You may all go outside now to play.

(Outside there was a hose coiled up near the shed door. Three children decided to use the hose to play fire fighters. They dragged it to a large fixed climbing structure. One child rushes inside and comes out wearing a hat.)

Damien: I'm the fireman!

Sue: I'm a fireman too. Just pretend I've got a hat.

Allan: Where's the fire?

Damien: In the house. (he points to the climbing structure. They are joined by Audrey. There is a lengthy discussion and Audrey crawls under the structure. It appears she is going to be rescued. The play is beginning.)

Teacher (calling in a loud voice): Time to wash hands for fruit time! Come on, everybody. Sue, Allan, Damien come on. Time for fruit.

The negotiated play, setting up the environment and determining the action had used up all the 'free time'. A short amount of time may mean, as in this case, that the play is stopped just as it is getting started. 'Free time' is often just not provided for in long enough periods. Christie and Wardle suggest that when this happens to children repeatedly they give up on group play 'and settle for less advanced forms of play that can be completed in shorter periods of time' (Christie & Wardle 1992, p. 29). Socio-dramatic play episodes need time to develop and evolve, and children need time to explore the possibilities. Only then will children revisit the play after a break as children did with the 'fishing play'.

How much time do you give children to develop and play out their play themes? It is vital that, as adults, we ask ourselves this because, as Creaser points out, 'play is central to the lives of all children. It is the natural behaviour through which children learn most effectively' (Creaser 1990, p. 13).

Necessary materials and resources

Since play develops as children themselves develop and acquire more experiences, so the way they use props will change. When children are just beginning to take on roles, they need materials and props that specify their use; for example, tea-sets, telephones, hair-rollers and toys on wheels. At this stage, it is unlikely that a tea-pot will be used as anything else, but as the child matures the tea pot may become an oil can and the hair-rollers become batteries for a space ship (Dau 1991, p. 78). Services, therefore, should have a mixture of structured and unstructured materials available.

Structured materials—those with specified uses—are important in all services and include dolls, prams, strollers, tea-sets, cooking utensils, brooms, telephones and so on. Much of this material relates, in the first instance, to early forms of socio-dramatic play around themes such as mothers and fathers but later may also be used in other ways and incorporated into other more complex play themes.

For the more complex stages of play children may still use structured material, but will also need unstructured materials that can become what they require for their play—for example, cardboard boxes and cylinders, fabric, rope and planks of wood. There is no, or little, cost attached to these materials—they simply need to be organised. A useful adjunct is paper of various sizes and writing implements. This encourages the development of literacy through play with, for instance, making a shop sign or train tickets or arranging speeding fines for offenders.

You may recall in the Introduction that Chris was able to introduce the play theme of camping quickly and seemingly easily. I asked her how she anticipated the need for camping materials. She reminded me that she always has had prop boxes in the storeroom and so she was able to go to the camping box and take out what she needed. Chris and her staff have, over a number of years, developed prop boxes, sometimes at their instigation and sometimes at the children's. I recall taking photos in the centre where Chris was working as a team leader at the time. When I arrived, she asked, 'What do you want the children to play?' I still remember my obviously puzzled look and lack of response. Chris came to my rescue, and said, 'We've got lots of prop boxes and whatever I bring out someone will play with.' We agreed on the post office box and, although I had been a little sceptical, within a very short time three children were involved in setting up a post office, Chris was a customer asking for stamps and the play had begun. This is a centre where children know their play is valued! 'How do they know that?' I asked Chris once, and her response was 'because I give them time to play, I give them props and material and because I can be playful too'.

Prop boxes can be a very useful tool to foster some children's play and are particularly helpful for the less imaginative. The post office prop box, for instance, contained stamp pad, rubber stamps, envelopes, pens, paper, scales, used stamps, glue, telephone and telephone directory. You are only limited by your imagination in developing props for children's play. Keep in mind, however, that experience comes first. Children who don't know about post offices will be less able to play that theme realistically than those who have seen how they work.

Reflecting diversity in resources

Should resources reflect diversity? The simple answer is 'yes'. While anti-bias education extends far beyond the provision of resources, teachers should consider setting up environments that represent diversity—which fits within an overall anti-bias approach. Young children are very interested in differences and similarities among people, and teachers can use resources to extend understanding of diversity issues. I am reminded of this story, told to me by Molly, about introducing diversity into children's play.

There are a number of children of Greek background in the service where Molly works. One of the fathers is a part-owner of a Greek restaurant, so Molly decided to talk to him about bringing a group of children to the restaurant. He agreed. After this visit, Molly wrote to the families of the children in her area asking for any resources, or advice on where to buy resources cheaply, that were specifically Greek and used in their homes. She explained this was so that a Greek restaurant could be set up in their area, and used this opportunity to reinforce the value of play in children's lives.

A week or so later Molly reminded the children again about their visit to the restaurant. Another group of children was to visit that afternoon. After the last of the children had gone home, Molly and another staff member set up the Greek restaurant in the dramatic play area. Children 'eating' Greek food, serving coffee from a Greek coffee pot and 'reading' the menu below brightly-coloured posters of Greece continued over a number of days. Molly, as one of the customers, was given lots of cups of coffee. Moussaka, and other dishes, became regular features in the menu.

I asked Chris how she reflects the diversity of the families in her service when selecting resources. She responded that children have many multicultural resources and materials to choose from. If the dramatic play area is a restaurant there will be knives, forks, spoons, bowls and saucepans, but also chopsticks and a wok, for example. I asked her if any of the children commented on the resources and she recalled what happened when she had introduced the wok into the dramatic play area. One of the children asked, 'what's that?' Chris explained, then realised that the child did not understand her explanation. As the centre is open-plan and the children can all see into the kitchen from a long stool built for that purpose, Chris called to the cook, 'Jen, when can we have some food cooked in the wok?' The next day those children could watch the food being cooked in a wok. The episode was another reminder that the experience must come before the play!

When selecting resources for children's socio-dramatic play, think about including ones that will be unique to some children and day-to-day resources for others. Consider, too, the importance of children trying out various roles. Does your hairdressing box, for example, include products used by both men and women? Do your resources encourage both girls and boys to be doctors, nurses, flight attendants, fire fighters and so on?

What about the dolls in the dramatic play area? Green suggests that 'anatomically correct dolls, which reflect diverse racial and ethnic identities, can make a difference in the classroom. Dolls with similar bodies and a variety of physical features such as different skin colours, eye shapes, hair and gender anatomy, help children gain familiarity and ease with diversity' (Green 1995, p. 19).

Here I'd like to sound a word of warning, however. Resources that reflect diversity are important in all services, but reflecting diversity goes far beyond the selection of resources. 'It involves eliminating stereotypical materials and resources, selecting anti-bias materials, using old material in creative ways, and creating visual displays which include images of all children and their families and which adequately reflect diversity.' (Green 1995, p. 18)

Neither should teachers be merely providers of props. To quote Boutte et al.:

> We urge teachers to remember the integral role they play in rein-
> forcing attitudinal multicultural (and anti-bias) competencies. The
> simple provision of materials without teacher guidance does little
> for . . . awareness. Children become more tolerant because mul-

ticultural (and anti–bias) activities are integrated daily rather than in isolated units. (Boutte et al. 1996, p. 39)

Conclusion

From research conducted by Creaser in 1990 there appears to be a recognisable and predictable sequences of events that lead to rich, complex children's play. As Molly showed, this involves:

- organising to go to a restaurant to have a real experience;
- gathering the props that help children adopt roles;
- setting up the scene with and without the children;
- joining in the play and role playing (an adult role such as a customer, never the baby);
- asking key questions of the players as you play with them.

In order to introduce a play-based program, teachers have to be prepared to change the power base, the environment and the schedule in order to allow children the control and freedom to build their own play space, and the time to develop child-directed, highly complex socio-dramatic play.

For further thought and discussion

1. Provide a daily free play period of one hour over the course of a week. Observe the results. Experiment with longer periods and observe the results.
2. The teacher in the fire fighter scenario could have considered alternatives to children having to go inside for fruit time. What would some alternatives be?
3. If you are planning a trip to the beach, how would you encourage children's socio-dramatic play following this excursion? What other excursions might you plan? Look closely at your own community. Where could you take children to extend their experience?
4. How much freedom do you allow for socio-dramatic play? Would you, for example, allow the children involved in a socio-dramatic play sequence to continue the play for 30 minutes, one hour, the morning or all day?

    Would you allow a 'cave' to be built inside? What would you do if the children wanted to bring in the outdoor blocks as part of their construction?

5. Assess the resources you have to support socio-dramatic play. Do you have dolls that reflect the diversity in the community? Have you avoided tokenism by having more than, for example, one black doll? Are there unstructured materials accessible for children and are they organised?
6. Re-read the list of tasks that a 'good early childhood teacher performs' which is in the introduction to this chapter. Think of examples of how you have instigated children's play, elaborated on children's play themes or provided the impetus for play.

References

Boutte, G., Van Scoy, I. & Hendley, S. 1996, 'Multicultural and non-sexist prop boxes', *Young Children*, Nov., pp. 34–9.

Creaser, B. 1990(a), *Rediscovering Pretend Play*, Australian Early Childhood Resource Booklet No. 4, Australian Early Childhood Association, Canberra.

Creaser, B. 1990(b), *Play Programming in Early Childhood Settings*, (unpublished).

Christie, J. & Wardle, F. 1992, 'How much time is needed for play?' *Young Children*, March, pp. 28–32.

Dau, E. 1991, 'Let's pretend: socio-dramatic play in early childhood', in Wright, S. (ed.), *The Arts in Early Childhood*, Prentice Hall, Sydney.

Green, R. 1995, 'Creating an Anti-Bias Environment' in Creaser, B. & Dau, E. (eds), 1995, *The Anti-Bias Approach in Early Childhood*, HarperEducational, Sydney.

Jones, E. & Reynolds, G. 1992, *The Play's the Thing: Teachers' Roles in Children's Play*, Teachers College Press, New York.

Jones, E. & Reynolds, G. 1997, *Master Players: Learning from Children at Play*, Teachers College Press, New York.

Smilansky, S. 1968, *The Effects of Socio-Dramatic Play on Disadvantaged Preschool Children*, Wiley, New York.

Smilansky, S. & Shefatya, L. 1990, *Facilitating Play: A Medium for Promoting Cognitive, Socio-Emotional and Academic Development in Young Children*, Psychosocial and Educational Publications, Gaithersburg.

Appendix

Exploring the correlation between *Child's Play* and the National Child Care Competency Standards

Helen Gibson

This appendix links the contents of the chapters in this book with the National Child Care Competency Standards. Readers with a particular interest in a topic may benefit from reading the unit/s of competence linked to that chapter; those using the Competency Standards for teaching or professional development will benefit from reading the chapter/s linked here with specific units of competence.

It is fascinating to note recurrent themes in this diverse body of work. Prevalent in many chapters is *PR14 Observe children and interpret observations*. Dockett, Fleer, MacNaughton, Creaser and Dau all address aspects of this unit of competence, either implicitly or explicitly. Another recurring theme is *IC4 Work collaboratively with children*. Creaser writes emphatically of the need to observe children and use that information to work more effectively and collaboratively with all children, especially those with additional needs.

Many contributors describe ways to *Support, foster and enhance children's development*. The experiences in a playground described by Berry would foster all aspects of children's development, particularly *FC7 Foster children's aesthetic and creative development*. Stonehouse encourages us to individualise the program for infants and toddlers to match their needs, interests and style and to give priority to their social-emotional needs; that is, *CN10 Support the emotional needs of children*. Harrison and Tegel provide stimulating ideas on ways to *Foster children's cognitive development (FC5)*, *Enhance the development of children's language development (FC11)* and *Promote the ethical understandings of children (FC20)*, all of which are particularly relevant to children who are gifted.

Stonehouse and Fasoli describe the benefits of *RF11 Work in partnerships with families to care for the child* and *RF12 Create links with*

community members and organisations. Fasoli and Bosisto with Howard illustrate the delights of *IC11 Implement and promote inclusive practices and policies.*

A link can be made between the approach taken by several authors and the Unit of Competence *SD10 Develop new approaches for providing service.* Fleer, MacNaughton, and Bosisto with Howard all illustrate the broad scope of this competence.

The following tables illustrate some aspects of the relationship between these chapters and the Competency Standards. It is a subjective view and it is not exhaustive. Its purpose is to explore the correlation between the chapters and standards, and to contribute to the ongoing debate about the nature and goals of early childhood services.

Table 1: Links between chapter contents (Part 1) and the National Child Care Competency Standards

	Foster children's development	*Provide for children's needs*	*Interactions with children*	*Relations with families*	*Programming*	*Workplace performance*	*Administrative and legal requirements*	*Service development*
Chapter 1 (Glover)	FC1–FC7				PR1–PR5			
Chapter 2 (Harley)			IC4 IC12		PR1–PR5 PR9			
Chapter 3 (Dockett)					PR12 PR14			SD10

Legend

FC1: Support the development of children; FC2: Foster the physical development of children; FC3: Foster the social development of children; FC4: Foster the emotional and psychological development of children; FC5: Foster children's cognitive development; FC6 Foster children's language development; FC7: Foster children's aesthetic and creative development.
IC4: Work collaboratively with children; IC12: Plan the inclusion of children with additional needs.
PR1: Facilitate play and leisure; PR2: Organise experiences for children; PR3: Observe children; PR4: Provide opportunities and experiences to enhance children's development; PR5: Enhance children's play and leisure; PR9: Use observations and recordings; PR12: Monitor and evaluate programs; PR14: Observe children and interpret observations.
SD10: Develop new approaches for providing service.

Table 2: Links between chapter contents (Part 2) and the National Child Care Competency Standards

	Foster children's development	Provide for children's needs	Interactions with children	Relations with families/communities	Programming	Workplace performance	Administrative and legal requirements	Service development
Chapter 4 (Fasoli)				RF11 RF12				SD10
Chapter 5 (Johns)	FC10 FC20	CN7	IC11					
Chapter 6 (Fleer)					PR3, PR9 PR12, PR14			SD10
Chapter 7 (MacNaughton)	FC4 FC20	CN20	IC11 IC14		PR3–PR9 PR12, PR14			SD10
Chapter 8 (Harrison & Tegel)	FC1–FC7 FC11 & FC20				PR1–PR5			
Chapter 9 (Creaser)	FC4	CN7 CN20	IC1 IC4	RF11	PR3, PR4 PR9 PR12–PR14			

Legend

FC1: Support the development of children; FC2: Foster the physical development of children; FC3: Foster the social development of children; FC4: Foster the emotional and psychological development of children; FC5: Foster children's cognitive development; FC6: Foster children's language development; FC7: Foster children's aesthetic and creative development; FC10: Enhance the emotional and psychological development of children; FC11: Enhance the development of children's language; FC20: Promote the ethical understandings of children; CN7: Foster children's self-help skills; CN20: Advocate for the rights and needs of children.

IC1: Interact positively with children; IC4: Work collaboratively with children; IC11: Implement and promote inclusive practices and policies; IC14: Facilitate children's communication skills.

RF11: Work in partnerships with families to care for the child; RF12: Create links with community members and organisations.

PR1: Facilitate play and leisure; PR2: Organise experiences for children; PR3: Observe children; PR4: Provide opportunities and experiences to enhance children's development; PR5: Enhance children's play and leisure; PR9: Use observations and recordings; PR12: Monitor and evaluate programs; PR14: Observe children and interpret observations.

SD10: Develop new approaches for providing service.

Table 3: Links between chapter contents (Part 3) and the National Child Care Competency Standards

	Foster children's development	Provide for children's needs	Interactions with children	Relations with families/ communities	Programming	Workplace performance	Administrative and legal requirements	Service development
Chapter 10 (Berry)	FC1–FC7				PR1 PR2			
Chapter 11 (Stonehouse)	FC1–FC7	CN10	IC1 IC4	PF11	PR3–PR5 PR9 PR14			
Chapter 12 (Bosisto & Howard)	FC3–FC5 FC10, FC11 FC20	CN10	IC11 IC12		PR2–PR4 PR10	WP2, WP3		SD10
Chapter 13 (Dau)	FC6 FC11				PR3–PR5 PR9 PR14			

Legend

FC1: Support the development of children; FC2: Foster the physical development of children; FC3: Foster the social development of children; FC4: Foster the emotional and psychological development of children; FC5: Foster children's cognitive development; FC6: Foster children's language development; FC7: Foster children's aesthetic and creative development; FC10: Enhance the emotional and psychological development of children; FC11: Enhance the development of children's language; FC20: Promote the ethical understandings of children.

CN10: Support the emotional needs of children.

IC1: Interact positively with children; IC4: Work collaboratively with children; IC11: Implement and promote inclusive policies and practices; IC12: Plan the inclusion of children with additional needs.

RF11: Work in partnerships with families to care for the child; RF12: Create links with community members and organisations.

PR1: Facilitate play and leisure; PR2: Organise experiences for children; PR3: Observe children; PR4: Provide opportunities and experiences to enhance children's development; PR5: Enhance children's play and leisure; PR9: Use observations and records; PR10: Facilitate the design of programs of the service; PR14: Observe children and interpret observations.

WP2: Contribute to the team; WP3: Develop own performance; SD10: Develop new approaches for providing service.

Index

A

ABC Task Force, 171, 172
Aboriginal children
    characteristics of play, 61–5, 73
    developmental theories, 68, 70, 72
    planning play, 60–1
Aboriginal people, 54–7
adults
    as architects of the environment,
        152–3, 157
    attitudes towards play, 13–14, 98
    role in children's play, 23–4, 153–4,
        155, 157, 158
    role in socio-dramatic play, 187
    role in supporting gifted children,
        102–3, 107, 108
anthropological studies, 74, 75
anti-bias
    checklist, 181–5
    curriculum, 167
    resource provision, 199–201
    under-three-year-olds, 160
Anti-bias Approach in Early Childhood:
        by B. Creaser & E. Dau, 166
*Anti-Bias Curriculum: Tools for
        Empowering Young Children:* by L.
        Derman-Sparks, 167
Anti-Bias Curriculum Task Force, 167
anti-bias research
    data collection, 168–71
    family responses, 177–9
    findings, 175–7
    interviews, 171–2
    parent involvement, 172–3
    session structure, 173–5
    staff involvement, 172

B

babies
    adults' role in play, 133–4, 152–3,
        155, 157, 158
    characteristics of play, 156
    essence of play, 154
    foundation for play, 159
    keys to programming, 161–2
    Melbourne Lady Gowrie Child
        Centre program, 154, 155
    planning play, 158–9
    play difference with older children,
        156–7
body in play, 19–20
Bosisto, Kerry, 164–6
Brodrick, Fiona, 153–5, 158–61, 162
Butler, Dorothy, 129–30

C

Canella, G., 39
capacity to play, 24–6
charts, 190–1
children. *see also* babies; toddlers
    development, 8–12
    learning from play, 5, 8–9
    play types, 187–8
children with disabilities. *see*
        special-needs children
cognitive conflict, 39
cognitive development, 11, 32, 34–6
competency-based training, 135
concept formation, 11
conceptualisation of play, 69–70
Creaser, Barbara, 28, 36, 43, 111, 201
creativity, 106–7
critical thinking, 167, 168
cross-cultural checklist, 181–5
cross-cultural differences, 76–7
cross-cultural studies, 71–2
cubbyhouse, 139, 142, 149
curriculum framework, 167

D

danger in play, 82, 84
Dau, Elizabeth, 164, 166

day care, 158
Derman-Sparks, Louise, 167, 171, 172, 179, 180
developmental paradigm, 19–23, 24
  conceptual shifts, 69–70
developmental theories
  cross-cultural relevance, 68
disabled children. *see also* special-needs children
dolls. *see* persona dolls
dramatic play, 16, 17–18, 26. *see also* socio-dramatic play
  crossing gender boundaries, 81–93
  objects used, 37
  power, 81–4
  value, 91–3
dramatist children, 187, 193, 194
dynamic play, 91–3

E
early childhood educators
  gender boundaries, 90–1
  role, 23–4
early readers, 104
embodiment, 19–20, 23
emotional development, 10–11
ethnographic studies, 74, 75, 78
explorer children, 188

F
Feitelson, D., 68, 71, 74, 75
Foucault, Michel, 81, 82
free play, 70–1, 106, 196
Fun Bus (NT), 53, 54

G
Gaskins, S., 75
gender boundaries, crossing
  case example, 85–9
  girls, 85, 89
  minimising risks, 90–1
gifted children
  advanced literacy, 107–8
  attitudes towards, 98
  characteristics, 98, 100, 106
  complex language, 107–8
  connections with like-minded peers, 105

exploring complex issues, 104–5
  numeracy skills, 107, 108
  opportunities for play, 101–2, 103, 106–7
  play patterns, 99–100
  resources, 104
  role of supportive adults, 102–3, 107, 108
  time for play, 105
giftedness, 97
Göncü, A., 39–40, 75

H
Hamilton, A., 72, 73
Howard, Anne, 164, 165, 166
humour, 64

I
intersubjectivity, 39–41
introversion, 99

J
J. B. Cleland Kindergarten, Adelaide, 167
Jennings, S., 19, 20

K
knowledge, 7, 10

L
Lady Gowrie Child Centre, Melbourne, 154, 155
Leach, Darlene, 153–5, 158–61, 162
learning, 8–9
Levin, D., 6, 11, 14
Lillian de Lissa Action Research Scholarship, 167
literature and learning centres, 108

M
materials for play, 22, 197–8
McGinnis, Kathleen, 94
mental representation, 37–8, 39, 41
motor skills, 12
multicultural consciousness-raising, 53–8
multiculturalism, 160

N

National Child Care Competency Standards, 135, 203–9
non-players, 18

O

observation, 32, 189, 192

P

parent's attitudes, 13–14
Parten, M., 29, 34, 35, 36, 41, 61, 72, 78
peer relationships, 9
persona dolls, 164
  anti-bias research project, 168–80
  home visits, 177–9
Persona Dolls: Anti-Bias in Action: by K. Jones, 166
physical development, 12
Piaget, J.
  developmental theory, 61, 69, 72, 78
  play categories, 29, 32, 34, 35, 36, 38, 39, 41
play
  categories, 32–6, 41
  constructivist perspective, 6–14
  cultural characteristics, 73–6
  defining, 31–2, 76
  definition, 16
  devaluing, 5, 12, 13
  function, 5
  interpreting, 32
  negative aspects, 92–3
  observing, 32, 189, 192
  opportunities for gifted children, 101
  social factors changing, 13
  types, 68–9
play fighting, 64
play group services
  cultural relevance, 53–8
play platform, 142–4
play process, 6
play styles, 36
playground
  features, 139–49
  plan, 138
  purpose, 137

redevelopment, 137–49
power in play, 81–2, 84
  case examples, 82–3
Prescott, Elizabeth, 111
pretend play. *see* dramatic play
Prime Times: A Handbook of Excellence in Infant and Toddler Care, 153
projective materials, 22
projective play, 21–2, 23

R

racial awareness research, 167, 168–80
racial bias, 169
racism, 171
relationships
  peer, 9
  understanding, 11
representational play, 68, 71, 73, 74, 76, 77
responsibility, 64, 65
risk in play, 81, 84, 85. *see also* gender boundaries, crossing minimisation, 81, 91
risk-taking, 61–3
role play, 16, 22–3

S

self-esteem, 10–11
sensory materials, 22
Smilansky, S., 32, 35, 36, 41, 68, 69, 73, 74, 78
social behaviour rules, 9
social categories of play, 32–6, 41
social development, 9–10
socio-dramatic play. *see also* dramatic play
  adults' role, 187
  charts, 190–1
  elements, 69
  gifted children, 106
  observing, 189, 192
  planning, 192–4
  real-life experiences, 194–6
  resources, 197–201
  time allocation, 196–7
specialist consultants, 112
special-needs children

case example: Jorge, 122–5
case example: Maria, 116–21,
   122
characteristics, 125–6
dramatic play, 25–6
mainstreaming strategies, 129
schools, 112–16
teachers of, 127–8
spectator children, 188
survival mechanism, 63–4
swings, 144–5
symbolic thought, 11

T
teachers. *see also* early childhood
   educators
charactistics of good, 188
definition, 111
role in curriculum, 167–8
of special-needs children, 112,
   127–8
television, 5, 6, 12
theory of mind, 37
thinking, 41–3
toddlers

adults' role in play, 152–3, 155, 157,
   158
characteristics of play, 156
essence of play, 154
foundation for play, 159
Melbourne Lady Gowrie Child
   Centre program, 154, 155
planning play, 158–9
play difference with older children,
   156–7
turtle hunting, 55–7

U
under-three-year-olds. *see* babies;
   toddlers

V
Vygotsky, L., 29, 32–3, 39, 72
free play, 70–1

W
Western perspective, 36
application to non-Western cultures,
   68, 70, 73–6

Young Children's Behaviour
Practical Approaches for Caregivers and Teachers
LOUISE PORTER

When adults care for and educate very young children, they aim to foster the children's autonomy and self-management. When staff respond to young children's disruptive behaviour however, they often find themselves using methods that demand the children do as they are told. These two approaches are in obvious conflict.

In *Young Children's Behaviour—Practical Approaches for Caregivers and Teachers*, Louise Porter aims to:

• provide practical suggestions for responding to young children's behaviour, using a child-centred perspective that is consistent with the educational goals of staff;
• suggest behaviour management techniques that safeguard the emotional needs of the child as well as the rights of other children and adults in the group;
• embed these concepts within a clear and accessible theoretical framework

Drawing on her experience as a child psychologist and as an academic in early childhood education at Flinders University in Adelaide, Louise Porter has produced a resource that is both highly practical and theoretically sound. Students, caregivers and teachers will benefit from the conversational style and step-by-step approach. Comprehensive appendices include quality guidelines, creative activities, and a list of readings that have been carefully selected to address challenging issues for both adult and child.

0-86433-143-6

Children with Disabilities, 4ed.

Edited by
MARK L. BATSHAW, M.D.

Professionals, families and students can rely on this fully illustrated, comprehensive resource for all of their disability reference needs. Along with extensive coverage of genetics, heredity, pre– and post–natal development, specific disabilities, family roles, and intervention, this edition features new chapters on substance abuse, AIDS, Down syndrome, fragile X syndrome, behaviour management, transitions to adulthood, and health care in the 21st century. It also reveals the causes of many conditions that can lead to developmental disabilities. The convenient selection of appendices includes a new one that describes the properties and uses of a wide variety of medications.

For a personal, professional or academic use, this informative classic has a place on the desk of everyone who works with, cares for, or loves a child with disabilities.

1-55766-293-2

The Australian Early Childhood Association

The Australian Early Childhood Association Inc. (AECA) is a national peak non-government organisation acting in the interests of young children aged from birth to eight years of age, and for older children in outside school hours care. AECA is based in Canberra, ACT.

AECA actively promotes the provision of high-quality services for all young children and their families, and supports the important role of parents.

AECA also has an important role as the national umbrella organisation for Children's Services. AECA sees this task as supporting the advocacy role of the child care sector as a whole, without undermining the rights of each specialist organisation to operate and speak independently.

AECA is a leading specialist publisher of early childhood literature. AECA produces the *Australian Journal of Early Childhood*, *Every Child* magazine, the AECA Research in Practice series, newsletter and special titles.

AECA also markets resources on early childhood topics from other companies and organisations.

For further information on AECA's resources

Telephone: (02) 6241 6900
Facsimile: (02) 6241 5547
Email: national@aeca.org.au
Website: www.aeca.org.au
or write to:
AECA
PO Box 105
Watson, ACT 2602